Teens, Crime, and the Community

Teens, Crime, and the Community

Education and Action for Safer Schools and Neighborhoods

A joint publication of the National Institute for Citizen Education in the Law and the National Crime Prevention Council

National Institute for Citizen Education in the Law
Edward T. McMahon
Judith A. Zimmer

National Crime Prevention Council
Terence W. Modglin
Jean F. O'Neil

Contributing Writer
Theresa Kelly

WEST PUBLISHING COMPANY
St. Paul   New York   Los Angeles   San Francisco

Copy Editing: Nancy Palmer-Jones
Figure Illustration: Miyake Illustration
Art Illustration: Francis E. Washington, Jr.
Indexing: Linda Cupp

Photo Credits:

Page 15, Bob Daemmrich, Stock, Boston; page 26, Bob Daemmrich, Stock, Boston; page 31, Jim Whitmer, Stock, Boston; page 53, Jean F. O'Neil, National Crime Prevention Council; page 68, Jerry Howard, Stock, Boston; page 128, Debbie Dreiling, National Crime Prevention Council; page 140, Harvey Bilt, International Photographers Association; page 161, PhotoEdit; page 171, Frank Siteman, Stock, Boston; page 174, John Coletti, Stock, Boston; page 187, Harvey Bilt, International Photographers Association.

This book was prepared under Grant No. 90-JD-CX-K002(S-1), from the Office of Juvenile Justice and Delinquency Prevention, Office of Justice Programs, U.S. Department of Justice. Points of view or opinions in this document are those of the authors and do not necessarily represent official positions or policies of the U.S. Department of Justice.

Library of Congress Cataloging-in-Publication Data

Teens, crime, and the community : education and action for safer schools and neighborhoods / National Institute for Citizen Education in the Law, National Crime Prevention Council.—2nd ed.
       p.   cm.
    Includes index.
    ISBN 0-314-89357-1 (soft)
    1. Students—United States—Crimes against. 2. Youth—United States—Crimes against. 3. Juvenile delinquency—United States. 4. Crime prevention—United States. I. National Institute for Citizen Education in the Law (U.S.) II. National Crime Prevention Council (U.S.)
HV6250.4.S78T4   1992
364.3'6'0973—dc20

                                                                91-44645
                                                                CIP

Preface

Crime continues to be one of the most difficult social problems faced by the United States. In surveys and polls it always emerges as one of people's principal concerns; it elects and defeats seekers of public office; it consistently incites debate with regard to the budget. The American public often views crime as a litmus test of the nation's condition.

Teenagers play a critical role in the crime situation. Though it is well known that teenagers commit a disproportionate number of crimes in our country, it is not well known that teenagers are also the age group most victimized by personal crimes. Also not well recognized is the enormous amount of energy and talent teens can contribute to making their communities safer.

The National Institute for Citizen Education in the Law (NICEL) and the National Crime Prevention Council (NCPC) joined forces in 1985 to educate secondary school students about ways they could make themselves, their families, their friends, and their communities safer and better. Since that time, persons in forty states have participated in the *Teens, Crime, and the Community* initiative.

NICEL brings to the partnership its talent for transforming dry legal issues into dynamic and enjoyable learning experiences through law-related education. NCPC brings its knowledge of effective crime prevention programming, its ability to create successful local partnerships, and its experience in making communities aware that young people can be talented crime prevention resources.

This partnership has resulted in a twofold national initiative. First, the *Teens, Crime, and the Community* curriculum advances the notion that teens can contribute energy and talent to the improvement of their communities. Starting with the first chapter ("Teens and Crime Prevention") and continuing throughout the entire text, students are encouraged to examine crime in their schools and communities and to apply the prevention lessons they learn.

Secondly, *Teens, Crime, and the Community* challenges teens to make the places where they live, work, and attend school safer and more caring. Community projects, led by students working with adults, give each young participant a strong sense of self, as a contributing member of the community with a vested interest in its future.

The whole *Teens, Crime, and the Community* initiative is based on the premise that crime victimizes us individually and collectively, and that crime prevention solutions involve both watching out and helping out.

From its inception in early 1985, the enterprise has grown remarkably. By the end of 1991, more than 300,000 teens will have participated, in classrooms, student councils, youth membership organizations, juvenile justice settings, and Native American reservations.

The effort can—and should—grow. We owe it to our youth and to our society.

Changes in this Edition

This edition of *Teens, Crime and the Community: Education and Action for Safer Schools and Neighborhoods* builds upon the popularity of earlier editions. Incorporating their best features, this edition provides new information, practical advice, and competency-building activities designed to enable students to understand the civic problem of crime, and to take action to prevent it.

This edition reflects new information, including updated crime statistics; new considerations, such as loss of community due to drug trafficking; and perspectives that we believe are essential to the understanding and prevention of crime in the early 1990s. New material in the book includes:

- Materials on how to prevent rape and assault (Chapter 2, "Victims of Crime");
- Sections on the relationships between violent crime and drugs, gangs, and handguns (Chapter 3, "Violent Crime");
- A section on intellectual and computer crime (Chapter 4, "Property Crime and Vandalism");
- An entirely new chapter on conflict management, a concept as well as a set of skills which many government officials and citizens believe are crucial to reducing violence and crime (Chapter 6, "Conflict Management");
- A discussion of date rape (Chapter 8, "Acquaintance Rape");
- An expanded discussion of problems caused by substance abuse (Chapter 9, "Substance Abuse and Drug Trafficking");
- A new, large section on the risks of local drug trafficking, a pernicious crime problem often overlooked in addressing our nation's drug problems (Chapter 9, "Substance Abuse and Drug Trafficking");
- Expanded information on laws regarding drunk driving, many of which have been successful in reducing fatalities and injuries (Chapter 10, "Drunk Driving");
- More extensive information on the costs of shoplifting to businesses, teens, and the community (Chapter 11, "Shoplifting").

Approach

Teens, Crime, and the Community presents practical information and problem-solving opportunities that help students develop the knowledge and skills necessary to deal with crime issues. The curriculum includes case studies, surveys, role-plays, small group exercises, and visual analysis activities. For optimal results, *Teens, Crime, and the Community* requires the participation of community resource people, such as police officers and lawyers. It also requires student involvement in the design and execution of hands-on projects such as teaching younger children, conducting neighborhood watches, and developing conflict management programs. This approach allows students to be active participants in their own education. In this way, we hope to promote

in students the willingness and capability to participate effectively in legal and political systems.

Utilization

In a number of school districts, *Teens, Crime, and the Community* has been incorporated into introductory social studies or law-related education courses. In other areas, it has been used in more advanced academic contexts, with students undertaking more in-depth research projects. As of 1991, approximately 300,000 students in 40 states have studied the text in a variety of curriculum formats.

Value

Properly used, *Teens, Crime, and the Community* has been found to contribute to programs that reduce crime and juvenile delinquency. Teachers should note that a separate, comprehensive Teacher's Manual and a supplemental Test Bank are available from the publisher.

We will continue to strive to improve the program. Your thoughts and comments are always welcome.

Edward O'Brien
Co-Director
National Institute for Citizen Education in the Law

John A. Calhoun
Executive Director
National Crime Prevention Council

Washington, D.C.
December, 1991

The Partners

Teens, Crime, and the Community is the product of a unique partnership of the National Institute for Citizen Education in the Law and the National Crime Prevention Council. This partnership was forged in 1985 under the leadership of Terry Donahue of the Office of Juvenile Justice and Delinquency Prevention, U.S. Department of Justice.

National Institute for Citizen Education in the Law (NICEL)

The Institute grew out of a Georgetown University Law Center program, launched in 1971, in which law students teach practical law courses in District of Columbia high schools, juvenile and adult correctional institutions, and a number of community-based settings.

NICEL was created to promote increased opportunities for citizens to learn about the law. It develops curricula, trains teachers, and develops and replicates programs internationally (some NICEL programs have been replicated in South Africa, Lesotho, Israel, Ecuador, Chile, and the Philippines). It also provides technical assistance and curriculum materials to law schools, school systems, departments of corrections, juvenile justice agencies, bar associations, legal service and community organizations, state and local governments, and other groups and individuals interested in establishing law-related education programs. Through its national clearinghouse, NICEL distributes lists of its materials and services as well as technical assistance papers that guide practitioners in the replication of its program models. NICEL also provides assistance for programs at the elementary school level.

In addition to *Teens, Crime, and the Community*, NICEL publishes *Street Law*, the most popular law-related education text in the nation, and many other books and publications.

For further information or assistance, please contact:

National Institute for Citizen Education in the
  Law
711 G Street, S.E.
Washington, D.C. 20003
(202) 546-6644
TDD: (202) 546-7591
FAX: (202) 546-6649

National Crime Prevention Council (NCPC)

The National Crime Prevention Council has a twofold mission: to teach individuals of all ages how to reduce their risks of being victimized, and to energize citizens to look beyond self-protection and involve themselves in neighborhood- and community-wide actions that attack the causes of crime. NCPC does this through:

- The powerful symbol of McGruff, the Crime Dog, and the "Take a Bite Out of Crime" public service advertising campaign;
- High-quality educational materials of all types, including books, booklets, brochures, kits, and posters;

- Demonstration programs in which youths, community services, churches, and schools test theories in the day-to-day world and provide information vital to the future of crime prevention and the community;
- Publication of program and policy guides based on results of demonstration programs;
- Training for national, state, and local crime prevention practitioners, community organizations, and youth groups;
- An unparalleled network of citizens, professionals, and organizations that implement crime prevention programs at the grassroots level;
- The Crime Prevention Coalition, 136 organizations joined to fight crime and build community. Member organizations include Boys' and Girls' Clubs of America, Urban League, National PTA, American Association of Retired People, International Association Chiefs of Police, all four branches of the military, and more than 60 state organizations; NCPC serves as its secretariat.

Since its inception, NCPC has emphasized youth-led crime prevention programs. It has operated a number of national youth demonstration programs and has published a number of other important youth-oriented books such as *Making a Difference: Young People in Community Crime Prevention* (1985); *Reaching Out: School-Based Community Service Programs* (1988); *Charting Success: A Workbook for Developing Crime Prevention and Other Community Service Projects* (1989); *Changing Perspectives: Youth as Resources* (1990); and *Teen Power, Don't Fight Drugs Without It!* (1991). NCPC has also published a large number of kits of reproducible program materials for youths.

For further information or assistance, please contact:

National Crime Prevention Council
1700 K Street, N.W., 2nd Floor
Washington, D.C. 20006
(202) 466-6272
FAX: (202) 296-1356

Acknowledgements

The authors gratefully acknowledge the many teachers, law enforcement officers, law students, and attorneys who have assisted in the development of our curriculum materials. Over the years, many people have provided valuable field-testing, research, editorial assistance, encouragement, and support. We can name only a few in the space below, but we appreciate the efforts of all who have worked with us.

Judy Zimmer of NICEL and Jean O'Neil and Terry Modglin of NCPC continued as authors of this text edition. Theresa Kelly served well as a co-author for this edition during her tenure with NCPC. Co-author Ed McMahon's work was part of the core of the first, self-published edition of the text; we gratefully acknowledge his contribution.

Also gratefully acknowledged is the hard work and dedication of a number of NCPC's Youth Unit staff, including Jonann Wild, who from 1989 operated the national demonstrations which piloted many of the new materials in this edition; Debbie Dreiling, who surveyed teachers and crime prevention practitioners for their observations on the textbook and developed a national promotion strategy; Judy Kirby, whose efficient operations work helped to make this and other documents possible; and teen leaders Dan Altman and David Singh, who also tested materials in presentations, and provided research assistance.

We want especially to acknowledge the help and support of Lee Arbetman and Mary Curd Larkin, NICEL's Associate Directors. The chapter on conflict management had its genesis in work done at the Law and Public Service Magnet High School in Cleveland, Ohio. In 1982-83, high school students working with Judy Zimmer established a pioneering school-based mediation program and worked with elementary school conflict managers. In addition, special thanks for feedback on the conflict management chapter are due to Edna Povich and Kathy Owen of the Center for Dispute Settlement; Annette Townley, Executive Director of National Association for Mediation in Education; and Beth Green and Natalie Johnson.

Dedicated local leaders—teachers, law enforcement officers, civilian crime prevention leaders—prompted us to critique certain aspects of the previous edition, develop new ideas and materials, and test theories and strategies for this edition. We would especially like to thank Lewis Colson of Detroit, Michigan, for his work in further developing the action components of the program; Judy Parker of the D.C. Center for Citizen Education in the Law; David Trevaskis and Barbara Moses of Philadelphia, Pennsylvania, for their work in adapting the program to a student council setting; Detective Ray Bilbrey of Dallas, Texas, one of the program's pioneers, for his development of the role of resource persons in the program;

Maria Cedeño of Miami, Florida, for her work in general and adaptations in working with immigrant populations; Pat Miljanich of San Francisco, who developed the very elaborate school adaptation of the curriculum; Kip Lowe of the California Youth Authority, who developed a similarly elaborate adaptation for a juvenile justice setting; and SPEC Associates of Detroit, Michigan, whose evaluation work has helped us sharpen the curriculum.

NCPC and NICEL also wish gratefully to acknowledge the trainer corps and the rural school, juvenile justice, and Native American demonstration sites of the early 1990s, which have provided helpful suggestions.

For this edition, West Publishing undertook a review process that involved teachers and others across the country. We appreciate the generous efforts of:

Janet Hunter
Owens Valley High School

Al Glickman
South Miami Junior High School

Aaron Banks
Gorton High School

Alan Fox
Roosevelt High School

Gary James
Nether Providence Middle School

Don King
Central High School

The Office of Juvenile Justice and Delinquency Prevention (OJJDP), Office of Justice Programs, U.S. Department of Justice is the institution that provided the resources that have made the *Teens, Crime, and the Community* program a national reality. Terry Donahue, Ben Shapiro, Doug Dodge, and Travis Cain were the OJJDP officers whose interest, hard work, and insights improved the program, and who deserve our thanks.

In addition to OJJDP, a number of private foundations made the spread of the program possible and enabled NICEL and NCPC to test materials for this edition. Private funders of the program include:

W.K. Kellogg Foundation
The Prudential Foundation
The Morris Goldseker Foundation of Maryland
The Public Welfare Foundation

Eugene and Agnes Meyer Foundation
Gwendolyn Cafritz Foundation
The April Trust of Washington, D.C.
The Hardesty Foundation
The San Francisco Foundation
Koret Foundation
Chevron U.S.A., Inc.
Walter and Elise Haas Fund

Over the years, many agencies and organizations have helped to make possible the work of the National Institute for Citizen Education in the Law. We appreciate their support and acknowledge their assistance. We particularly wish to thank the following for their contributions:

Corporate/Foundation:

Batchelor Foundation, Inc.
Cora and John Davis Foundation
Covington & Burling Foundation
Cypen & Cypen
Dade Community Foundation
Eugene and Agnes E. Meyer Foundation
Exxon Corporation
Holland & Knight
International Business Machines
Morrison and Foerster
O'Connor & Hannan
Ruden, Barnett, McClosky, Smith, Schuster & Russell, P.A.
Sterling Drug, Inc.
U.S. Trust Company of New York
West Publishing Company
Xerox Corporation

Individuals:

Jacqueline Allee
Aggie Alvez
Lee Arbetman
Clyde Atkins
Lowell Beck
William Bell
Lee Roy Black
Jennifer Bloom
Rebecca Bond
David Brink
Thomas T. Cobb
Lawrence Dark
Tom Diemer
Charles Douglas
Gretchen Dykstra
Beth Farnbach
Robert Floyd
Mark Gelber
Brenda Girton
Ruth Gutstein
Katherine Hagen
Dean Hansell
William Henry
Roger Hewitt
A.P. and Mildred Hollingsworth
Mark Hulsey
T. Paine Kelly
Mary Larkin
Liane Levetan
Abelardo Menendez
Vivian Mills
Mark Murphy
Jason Newman
Edward O'Brien
Alan Page
Richard Parker
Lissa Pierce
Richard Pettigrew
E. Barrett Prettyman
Hon. William Pryor
Ramon Rasco
Janet Reno
James Rohloff
Debra Smith
Jerrol Tostrud
Mary Pat Toups
Sidney Tuchman
Dan Walbolt
Fay Williams
Judith Zimmer
Howard Zipser

National Leadership of the Partner Organizations

National Institute for Citizen Education in the Law National Advisory Committee

Chairperson:

Fay Williams
Attorney at Law
Indianapolis, IN

Materials Reprinted by Permission of NICEL

Chapter 1
Page 7, "What Causes Crime?" derived from *Street Law, A Course in Practical Law*, West Publishing, 1990.

Page 8, "Crime Ranking Strategy" taken from *Street Law, a Course in Practical Law*, West Publishing, 1990.

Page 17, "How to Report a Crime" derived from *Street Law, A Course in Practical Law*, West Publishing, 1990.

Page 18, "Are You a Good Witness?" used with permission of the Young Lawyers Section of the Bar Association of the District of Columbia.

Chapter 5
Page 74, "Criminal Justice Process" derived from *Street Law. A Course in Practical Law*, West Publishing, 1990.

Chapter 6
Page 104, mediation chart taken from *Street Law, A Course in Practical Law*, West Publishing, 1990.

Materials Reprinted by Permission of NCPC

Chapter 1

Page 2, "What Do You Know About Teens as Crime Victims?" derived from item of same name in *Charting Success: A Workbook for Developing Crime Prevention and Other Community Service Projects*, National Crime Prevention Council, 1989.

Page 12, "Because of a teenager, a crime didn't happen here," a message from the Crime Prevention Coalition and the Ad Council, © 1985, The Advertising Council.

Page 13, "Take a Look at Your School," derived from *Watch Out/Help Out: The Teen Action Kit*, National Crime Prevention Council, 1986.

Page 15, "Alone After School," derived from *Watch Out/Help Out: The Teen Action Kit*, National Crime Prevention Council, 1986.

Chapter 2

Page 35, "If a Friend Is Hit by Crime" taken directly from the article "So Your Friend's Been Hit by Crime?" in *Watch Out/Help Out: The Teen Action Kit*, National Crime Prevention Council, 1986.

Chapter 3

Pages 43-47, "Protecting Yourself from Robbery," "Protect Yourself in Transit," "Protect Yourself in Your Car," "Protect Yourself in Your Home," "If Someone Tries to Rape You," "If You Are the Victim of Rape," all contain a large portion of crime prevention materials which are derived from materials in *Watch Out/Help Out: The Teen Action Kit*, National Crime Prevention Council, 1986.

Page 42, "Tony thinks he's walking home alone . . . Tony's wrong," a message from the Crime Prevention Coalition and the Ad Council, © 1985, The Advertising Council.

Chapter 4

Page 65, "Preventing Theft" adapted from "Don't Be an Easy Mark for a Quick Rip Off," a brochure in *Watch Out/Help Out: The Teen Action Kit*, National Crime Prevention Council, 1986.

Page 67, "What Are the Costs and Who Are the Victims of Vandalism?" adapted from "Destroying Someone Else's Property Isn't Funny. It's Vandalism and It's a Crime," a brochure in *Watch Out/Help Out: The Teen Action Kit*, National Crime Prevention Council, 1986.

Chapter 9

Page 146, Adapted from an article in the *Washington Post*, page A1, February 16, 1989.

Page 148, "How Does Drug Trafficking Affect Teens?" *Substance Use and Dealing Among Inner-City Adolescent Males*, Harry P. Hatay, Paul Brownstein, David M. Altschuler, Louis H. Blair, Urban Institute Press, 1990.

Other Materials Reprinted by Permission

Chapter 7

Page 116, "12 alternatives to lashing out at your child," The National Committee for Prevention of Child Abuse, The Advertising Council.

Chapter 11

Page 180, "One way to ruin your future. (Count on it.)," © 1989, The Greater Washington Board of Trade.

Table of Contents

1   Teens and Crime Prevention   1

What Do You Know About Teens as
    Crime Victims?   2
What Is a Crime?   4
What Is the Difference Between a
    Felony and a Misdemeanor?   5
Violent Crime and Property Crime   5
What Causes Crime?   8
What Is Community Crime Prevention?   11
How Can Teens Prevent Crime?   13
Alone After School?   15
Reporting Crime   16
If a Crime Is Committed . . .   18
Reducing Opportunities for Crime   19
Holding the Offender Accountable   19
Attacking Social Ills   20

2   Victims of Crime   23

Who Are Victims?   24
Facts About Crime Victims   25
The Costs of Crime   27
The Case of Betty Jane Spencer   28
How Does Crime Affect Its Victims?   30
Advocacy for Victims   32
Victim/Witness Assistance and
    Crime Prevention   33
What Can You Do?   35
If a Friend Is Hit by Crime . . .   35

3   Violent Crime   39

What Is Violent Crime?   40
Protecting Yourself from Street Assaults   41

Protecting Yourself from Robbery   43
Preventing Rape   47
Assault: The Most Common Violent Crime   49
Drugs and Violent Crime   51
Gangs and Violent Crime   52
Handguns and Violent Crime   54
Reducing the Use of Handguns in Crime   56

4   Property Crime and Vandalism   59

What Is Property?   60
What Is Property Crime?   60
Which Are More Frequent, Property
    Crimes or Violent Crimes?   60
Types of Property Crime   61
How Are Teens Affected by Crimes of Theft?   63
Preventing Theft   65
Organizing Neighborhood Groups to
    Prevent Property Crime   66
Vandalism   67
"Invisible" Property Crime   71
A New Tool in Property Crime   71

5   Criminal and Juvenile Justice   73

What Is the Criminal Justice Process?   74
Criminal Law   74
Costs of Criminal Justice   75
Treatment of Victims   75
What Happens When a Crime Is Committed?   75
Juvenile Justice   85
Capital Punishment   89

6   Conflict Management   91

What Is Conflict?   92
Who Has the Energy to Resolve a Dispute?   93
What Role Do Courts Play in
    Conflict Management?   95
What Skills Are Involved in Personal
    Conflict Management?   96
Steps in Personal Conflict Management   102
Mediation   103

7   Child Abuse   107

What Is Child Abuse?   108
What Is Incest?   109
Characteristics of Sexual Assault and Incest 109
Emotional Abuse   110
Neglect   110
How Does the Public Feel
    About Child Abuse?   111
How Widespread Is Child Abuse?   111
What Are the Causes of Child Abuse?   113
Signs of Child Abuse   114
Preventing Child Abuse   115
Reporting Child Abuse   117
What Happens When Child Abuse
    Is Disclosed?   118
Support for Friends   119

8   Acquaintance Rape   121

What Is Acquaintance Rape?   122
The Effects of Acquaintance Rape on Victims 122
Myths and Facts About Sexual Assault   124
Causes of Date Rape   125
How You Can Protect Yourself   126
What if it Happens to You?   127
How to Help a Friend   127

**9   Substance Abuse and Drug
       Trafficking   131**

What Is Substance Abuse?   132
How Substance Abuse Causes Problems   133
What Is Addiction?   134
Physical Effects of Substance Abuse   135
Trends in Substance Abuse Among Teens   137

Looking at All the Costs   138
Decisions   139
Some Signs of Abuse   141
How to Talk to a Friend Who's in Trouble
    with Alcohol or Other Drugs   142
Teens and Substance Abuse Prevention   143
State and Federal Drug Laws   144
Lake Place   146
What Is Drug Trafficking?   148
How Does Drug Trafficking Affect Teens?   148
The Risks and Realities of Drug Trafficking 149
How Do Illegal Drugs and Trafficking
    Relate to Other Crime?   150
When Drug Traffickers Get Caught   151
How Does Drug Trafficking Affect the
    Community?   154

10   Drunk Driving   157

When Alcohol Kills   158
How Does Drunk Driving Relate to Teens? 160
Why Are Teens So Frequently Involved?   160
The Legal Drinking Age   162
How Does the Law Treat Drunk Driving?   163
Drinking and Driving Facts   166
How Does Drinking Alcohol Affect
    the Driver Physically?   166
Common Signs of Drunk Driving   167
Community Responses   170

11   Shoplifting   173

What Is Shoplifting?   174
What Is the Impact of Shoplifting
    on Businesses?   175
Who Shoplifts?   177
Costs of Shoplifting to the Community   178
How Does Shoplifting Affect Teens?   179
The Price of Being Caught   179
How Can Teens Stop Shoplifting?   180

Appendix: Designing a Project   185

Glossary   193

Index   197

1

Teens and Crime Prevention

Words to Know

crime
felony
misdemeanor
violent crime
property crime
larceny
forgery
crime prevention
restitution

Objectives

As a result of this chapter you should be able to:

- Define crime

- Explain the difference between a felony and a misdemeanor

- Discuss causes of crime and suggest solutions

- Describe crime and crime prevention in your community

- Explain the kinds of roles teens can play in crime prevention

- Identify the kinds and locations of crimes against teens

- Report a crime

Use Your Experience	What do you think is meant by the word *crime*? What crimes are most common in your community? What crimes are most commonly committed against teens in your community? What could you do to help solve the crime problem in your school? In your community?

What Do You Know About Teens as Crime Victims?

The following questions are based chiefly on data from an annual survey by the U.S. Department of Justice's Bureau of Justice Statistics on the nature and extent of crimes that victimize citizens and certain groups in particular.

Using a separate sheet of paper, write down your answers to these questions:

1. In which age category are persons most likely to be victims of crime?

    a. Elderly (65 and over)
    b. Middle-aged (35–49)
    c. Teenagers (12–19)

2. Are teenage males or females more likely to be victims of violent crime?

    a. Males
    b. Females
    c. Males and females are victimized equally.

3. For the three violent crimes of rape, robbery, and assault, are teens more or less likely than adults to be victimized by persons they know?

    a. Teens are less frequently victimized than adults by persons they know.
    b. Teens are more frequently victimized than adults by persons they know.
    c. Teens are victimized by persons they know at about the same rate as adults.

4. Of the violent crimes of homicide, rape, robbery, and assault, which is the most likely to be committed by someone the victim knows?

    a. Homicide
    b. Rape
    c. Robbery
    d. Assault

5. What percentage of deaths in the 15–24 age bracket are the result of injury, including crime-related injury?

   a. 79 percent (about four out of five)
   b. 28 percent (about one out of four)
   c. 50 percent

6. Which of the following age groups is least likely to report a crime?

   a. Elderly (65 and over)
   b. Teenagers (12–19)
   c. Middle-aged (35–49)

7. Which of these age groups had the largest number of murder victims in 1989?

   a. 35–39
   b. 25–34
   c. 20–24

Now read and discuss the following statistics. Then use the information to discuss the questions that follow.

1. Teenagers are crime's most frequent targets. Teens are victims of theft and violent crime at about twice the rate of the adult population age 20 and older. Younger teens (12–15 years old) have lower rates of violent crime than older teens (16–19), yet both groups have similar theft rates.*

2. Similar to the adult population, male teenagers experience higher rates of violent crime and theft than do female teens.*

3. Teenagers are more likely than adults to be victimized by people they know. The proportion of violent-crime victims who have reported that their offenders are known to them in some way (casual or close acquaintances, friends, relatives) is 49 percent for adults, 57 percent for older teenagers, and 68 percent for younger teenagers.*

4. Homicide is the violent crime in which the victim is most likely to know the offender in some way. According to the *Uniform Crime Reports* for 1987, which contain only reported crime, "three of every five murder victims in 1987 were related to (17 percent) or acquainted with (40 percent) their assailants." Among all female murder victims in 1987, 29 percent were slain by husbands or boyfriends. Six percent of the male victims were killed by wives or girlfriends. Arguments led to 37 percent of the murders in 1987.

*U.S. Department of Justice, *Teenage Victims: A National Crime Survey Report*, 1991.

5. Four out of five (79 percent) of all fatalities among persons ages 15–24 are the result of injury, according to a 1985 report by a commission of the National Research Council and the Institute of Medicine. Alcohol-related automobile accidents are the leading cause of deaths in this age group, followed by suicide and homicide. The use and abuse of alcoholic beverages influence the likelihood of virtually all types of injury. The report said, "Injury is the last major plague of the young."[1]

6. Teenagers are the age group least likely to report crime. Among teenagers, crimes against younger teens were less likely to be reported than crimes against older teens.[2]

7. Of those ages 20–24 in 1989, 3,159 were murdered. There were 2,001 teens ages 15–19 murdered in that year. Murders of older teens in 1989 outnumbered those of 35- to 39-year-olds by 79, and those of *all* Americans ages 55 and over by 92.

Your Turn

Here are some questions for class discussion:

1. Why are teens victims of crime more frequently than any other age group?
2. Why are teen males more frequent crime victims than teen females?
3. What kinds of things can teens do to decrease crime among people who know each other?
4. What are some ways to prevent homicide between those who know one another?
5. Why do teenagers report crime less often than do adults? How could teens be encouraged to report crimes more often?

What Is a Crime?

A **crime** is any behavior for which society has set a penalty. In the United States, the local, state, and federal governments define those acts that are crimes. The definition of a crime can change over time. The legislative bodies that make laws defining crime consist of people who are elected to represent citizens' views. As those views change, the exact definition of a given crime may change as well.

[1]National Academy of Science Press, *Injury in America: A Continuing Health Problem*, 1985.
[2]U.S. Department of Justice, *Teenage Victims: A National Crime Survey Report*, 1991.

Crime wears many faces. It may be committed by a career criminal burglarizing a house or by a teenager snatching a woman's purse. It may involve a youth who steals a car for a joyride or a car theft ring that takes it for later sale. It may be a drunk driver who kills a pedestrian, or a politician who takes a bribe. Crime may be committed by the professional who cheats on a tax return, the businessperson who steals money using a computer, or the mugger who robs people with a gun.

What Is the Difference Between a Felony and a Misdemeanor?

Criminal offenses are classified according to how they are handled by the criminal justice system. There are two classes of offenses: **felonies** and **misdemeanors**. Felonies are the more serious crimes. In most states felonies are defined as crimes punishable by a year or more in prison. Misdemeanors are offenses for which the penalty is imprisonment for less than one year. In some states, minor offenses, such as most traffic violations, are not considered misdemeanors although they are punishable by law.

Your Turn

1. What's the difference between a felony and a misdemeanor?
2. How does crime affect the way we live?

Violent Crime and Property Crime

Violent crime refers to acts such as assault, rape, and robbery that involve the use or threat of force against a person. Robbery is considered a violent crime even when no one is hurt, because it involves the threat of force.

Property crimes are acts that involve taking property illegally but that do not involve the use or threat of force against an individual. **Larceny**, **forgery**, and auto theft are examples of property crimes. Property crime also includes acts in which property is unlawfully damaged or destroyed, such as vandalism or arson.

Other common types of crime include fraud, alcohol-related offenses, sex offenses, and white-collar crime. Fraud involves intentionally misrepresenting information in order to take property belonging to someone else. Driving a vehicle while under the influence of alcohol or narcotics is a frequently committed crime. Sex offenses are violent crimes that involve forcing an unwilling person to engage in a sex act. White-collar crime involves using a position of power and trust to commit an illegal act.

Figure 1—Where violent crimes against teens occurred, 1985-1988

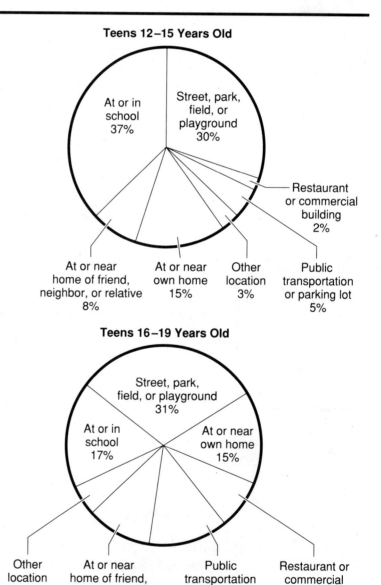

Teens 12–15 Years Old

At or in school 37%

Street, park, field, or playground 30%

Restaurant or commercial building 2%

At or near home of friend, neighbor, or relative 8%

At or near own home 15%

Other location 3%

Public transportation or parking lot 5%

Teens 16–19 Years Old

Street, park, field, or playground 31%

At or in school 17%

At or near own home 15%

Other location 5%

At or near home of friend, neighbor, or relative 11%

Public transportation or in parking lot 13%

Restaurant or commercial building 8%

Source: U.S. Department of Justice, *Teenage Victims: A National Crime Survey Report,* 1991.

Your Turn

Rank the ten offenses listed here from the most serious to the least serious based on your opinion, not on how serious the law now says they are. Rank the most serious (1), the second most serious (2), and so on, until you get to the least serious offense, which should be ranked (10). Then classify each as a felony, a misdemeanor, or not a crime at all. Explain the reasons for your decisions.

_7_   A. A factory knowingly dumps waste in a way that pollutes the water supply of a large city.

_9_   B. A person with a gun robs a victim of $40. No physical harm occurs.

_1_   C. A terrorist plants a bomb in an airport terminal. The bomb explodes and twenty people are killed.

_5_   D. A person forcibly rapes a teen, resulting in serious injury to the victim.

_2_   E. A person intentionally sets fire to a business, causing damages worth $250,000.

_6_   F. A person burglarizes a victim's home, taking property worth $150.

_4_   G. A drunk driver kills a teen pedestrian by driving an automobile recklessly.

_3_   H. A person sells crack cocaine to others.

_8_   I. A person shoplifts $80 worth of items from a department store.

_10_   J. A teen's car is vandalized in a parking lot.

Now, rank the seriousness of the following situations and determine where they would fit on your list of crimes.

8 B • As a student walks down the hall at school, a teen hits the student on the head and steals the victim's wallet.

10 C • One student says to another, "You will be beaten up after school if you don't give me your lunch money."

4 A • During an argument over use of the family car, a father knocks his son against a wall, breaking the son's arm.

Do you think society views crime more seriously when it is committed against an adult rather than a child or teen?

Your Turn

1. Based on the charts in Figure 1, where do most violent crimes against teenagers occur? Why?
2. Based on the statistics listed earlier in this chapter, which age group is most frequently victimized by violent crime? (This is called a crime victimization rate.) Which age group has the second highest victimization rate? Which age group has the lowest rate of victimization? How can you explain this?

In Your Community

1. Where do you feel safest? Least safe?
   a. Home
   b. School
   c. Going to or from school
   d. In your neighborhood
2. Describe the place where you feel the safest. Develop a list of factors that contribute to this sense of safety.

What Causes Crime?

Researchers in crime control and prevention give many reasons why people commit crime. But no theory is fully accepted by these professionals. The following sections describe some—but not all—of their theories.

Poverty and Unemployment

Many people believe crime is somehow connected to poverty. Some studies show that crime is highest among the poor and unemployed. The theory is that criminal behavior has less to do with the individual than it does with a person's circumstances.

However, there is evidence that crime cannot be totally explained by poverty. If poverty were the sole cause of crime, how would one explain why crime in the United States went up at a time when the number of people living in poverty was declining?

Some experts believe that the lack of money alone is not what causes crime in poor areas. They believe it is the change and instability in certain neighborhoods that lead to an atmosphere of tolerance or encouragement of criminal behavior.

Inadequate Police Protection and Permissive Courts

Some people believe that crime has gone up because the courts are soft on criminals. Critics call this "revolving-door justice." They say legal loopholes and lenient judges let dangerous criminals loose to prey on society. Critics say, "We should get tough on crime. We should hire more police and lock up more criminals for longer terms."

Adequate police protection does have something to do with crime control. However, studies show that simply hiring more police officers does not necessarily reduce crime, though it may reduce most citizens' fear of crime. Many experts say that simply putting people behind bars for longer terms will not reduce crime. They point out that the United States already locks up more people for longer terms than almost any other Western nation.

Locking up criminals or hiring more police officers is expensive. Studies show an average cost of $20,000 to $40,000 to lock up a person for one year. A national average of the cost of adding one police officer to a local police department is difficult to calculate due to regional and state cost-of-living variations. However, one survey of police departments in the mid-Atlantic states (Delaware, Maryland, New Jersey, New York, and Pennsylvania) revealed an estimated cost of $120,000 to $135,000 to hire, train, and otherwise fully equip one additional police officer.

Peer and Family Influence

Some people believe that criminal behavior is learned. They say it is learned by associating on a daily basis with other people who are involved in criminal activity. Through such contacts, a person learns a set of values and behaviors that encourage or condone crime.

Others say family influences are the cause of crime. For example, some parents aren't strict enough and don't teach their children to respect the law and the rights of others. Another argument is that crime is caused by emotional and family problems. Since the family is society's most important social group, it helps shape a person's behavior in later life. In other words, family problems or an unhappy childhood can lead to criminal behavior, according to this theory.

While no one doubts the crucial role of family and peers in a person's development, it is important to remember that children of the same parents, raised in the same surroundings, often follow opposite courses with respect to the law.

Size of Youth Population

Another theory is based on the idea that young people commit more crimes per person than any other age group. Young people ages 15–24 have the highest crime commission rate. In theory, then, if there are more young people, there is more crime.

After the late 1970s, the proportion of young people in the general population declined. From 1977 to 1986, the number of arrests of youths under the age of 18 declined by 12 percent. At the same time, there was a 39 percent increase in the number of arrests of those over age 18. These data suggest that crime rates can increase even when the proportion of youth in the population decreases. Therefore, it would seem that the age of the population cannot alone explain or predict crime.

Drug Abuse

The abuse of drugs is believed by many to be the chief cause of criminal activity. The study of drug use and its relationship to crime includes not only illegal drugs, such as cocaine and heroin, but alcohol as well.

Three main reasons are said to explain why drugs cause crime: the effects of the drug, which may cause violent or criminal behavior; the economic need of a user to support a drug habit, which leads to the need to obtain money quickly; and the basic competition risks that are part of the illegal drug-trafficking industry.

Surveys state that 60 percent of juveniles in state institutions were regular drug users before their arrest and that 40 percent of them committed the offense while under the influence. According to a 1989 study, 54 to 82 percent of the men arrested in 21 major cities for nondrug-related offenses, such as burglary, grand larceny, or assault, tested positive for at least one illegal drug. Alcohol plays a role in one-third of all child abuse cases and a large number of domestic violence cases.

The likelihood of becoming a victim also increases greatly with the use of alcohol or other drugs. For instance, a significant number of sexual assaults in which the victim knows the offender occur when the victim has used alcohol or other drugs. One recent study of murder victims found that 53 percent had alcohol or other drugs in their systems at the time of death.

Drug use, however, is not itself an explanation of crime. Some have suggested that the link is one of coincidence rather than of cause and effect. They suggest that individuals who are already involved in crime or who are likely to commit crime are also more inclined to become involved with drugs.

Other Theories

Many other reasons have been suggested to explain crime and its severity. These include easy access to handguns, the influence of television, the spread of pornography, and a decline in moral values.

As you can see, experts do not agree on the major causes of crime. It is likely that crime has many causes. Thinking about crime requires us to consider carefully all the suggested causes.

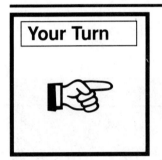

Your Turn

1. Briefly summarize each of the main theories on the causes of crime.
2. Which causes of crime do you think make the most sense? The least sense?
3. Rank each of the suggested causes of crime from the most important to the least important. Discuss your choices.

In Your Community

1. What do you think is the most serious crime problem in your community? In your school?
2. If you were the governor of your state, what would you do to solve the crime problem?

What Is Community Crime Prevention?

Crime doesn't just happen. It has causes, even if they are difficult to understand. In order to eliminate crime, society has tried to tackle its causes. Reducing and preventing crime are not only the jobs of police. Experience shows that it really makes a difference when citizens become involved.

When citizens in an area organize to develop programs to reduce crime and increase their sense of safety and security, those citizens are involved in community **crime prevention**. Community crime prevention programs show that people are serious about improving their neighborhoods and discouraging crime. These programs can be as personal and immediate as putting locks on windows or as broad as neighborhood cleanup campaigns.

Community involvement must include all community members—senior citizens, teens, parents, children, business owners, executives, police, and government. Greater community involvement increases the amount of energy directed at the problem. By getting to know each other better, neighbors can help make it more likely that their activities will be successful.

A community can be an entire town, a neighborhood, or a school. Students in many parts of the country have reached out to their classmates and their neighbors to help make the places where they live and attend school safer and more desirable.

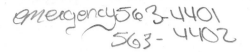
emergency 563-4401
563-4402

How Can Teens Prevent Crime?

Teens can prevent crime with the same strategies used by the general adult population. Self-protective actions include not carrying lots of cash or flashing it around, walking in well-lighted areas with friends rather than alone, and ensuring that your home's doors and windows are appropriately secured.

But remember that crime, and especially crime against teens, is often committed by people known to the victim. Thus, you need to develop good decision-making skills to deal with specific situations. One strategy for refining your decision-making skills is to "think it through," either by yourself or with friends, asking "what would I do if . . .?" questions.

For example, if you have to get from one place to another at night, try to figure out the safest way to travel. Can someone drive you or walk with you? Thinking and planning ahead may help to prevent a crime.

Protecting Your Community

Here are a few ideas about crime prevention from students active in their communities around the country:

- Anti-vandalism projects, like graffiti removal programs, in which students take the lead
- Student forums on drug abuse, drunk driving, runaways, suicide, or sexual abuse
- School crime watches to encourage students to report crime and to keep others from becoming victims
- Mediation programs that use neutral parties to help resolve disputes
- Projects that involve students in improving the school's physical environment and taking pride in its appearance
- Law classes to help students understand the legal system, as well as their own rights and responsibilities
- Community service projects that give students course credit, awards, or other formal recognition for their volunteer work in areas such as mental health, recreation, elder care in a nursing home, hospital health care, or library work.

Take a Look at Your School

One community that you are a part of is your school. No one—kids, teachers, principals—wants crimes to happen in school. But sometimes they do happen. Even a little vandalism or a few petty thefts threaten a school's well-being. They diminish the sense of pride and feeling of security that students need to have in their school. You and your friends can have roles in improving your school community.

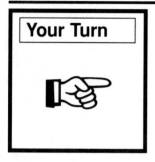

Your Turn

1.a. One night you see two unfamiliar teenagers throwing rocks through the windows of your local high school. Would you report them to the police? Why or why not? Would your answer be different if you knew the students?

   b. Suppose you saw the same teenagers vandalizing a neighbor's car. Would you report them to the police? Why or why not?

   c. Suppose you saw two teenagers vandalizing your own car. Would you report them to the police? Why or why not?

   d. Were your answers to Questions a through c consistent? Did you feel differently when the teens were vandalizing your car than when they were vandalizing your school? Why?

2.a. One afternoon at about 2:30 P.M., you see a blue van pull up in front of a neighbor's house. Two strange men get out of the van and walk to the rear of the house. You are suspicious because you know your neighbors are on vacation. What would you do? Does your answer change if you do not like your neighbors?

   b. If you call the police about the incident in Question 2a, what would you say? Role-play with a classmate a phone call between you and the police, discussing the situation in Question 2a.

   c. Have you ever witnessed a crime? What happened? What did you do? Brainstorm and discuss a list of reasons why a crime might go unreported.

In Your Community

Your class can conduct a survey about what students consider to be the most serious problems in your school. Once you have the survey results, list some resources and people that can help solve the problem.

The following questions may help you:

● Are teens expressing themselves on bathroom walls, doors, and hallways?

- Are the school grounds attractive, or do you see litter, overgrown shrubbery, and mud?
- Do fights break out often?
- Is having something stolen from a locker an everyday occurrence?
- Are drugs or alcohol being used by students in or near the school?
- Are some students afraid of others? Do some students avoid coming to school because of their fear?
- Does it take a while before a broken window, broken light—broken anything—gets fixed?

A clean, unlittered school is less likely to be vandalized and more likely to be respected by students.

Alone After School?

Many teens are by themselves after school until their parents return home from work. Some are baby-sitting for younger brothers or sisters. Here are some quick tips to keep you safe—and to keep your parents from worrying.

- Talk with your parents about what you can and should do before they get home.
- Know how to work all the door and window locks. Keep all doors locked when you are inside.

- Keep a list near the phone of key phone numbers—your parents at work, a neighbor, the police and fire departments, and the local poison control center.
- Check in with a parent at work as soon as you get home.
- Don't let anyone into the house or apartment unless you check with your parents first.
- Know the quickest ways to get out in case of fire. Get out immediately and call the fire department from a neighbor's house or a public phone.
- If you come home and things don't look quite right, don't go in. Go to a neighbor's home or a public phone and call the police.

Your Turn

1. One afternoon you're home alone talking to a friend on the phone when the doorbell rings. A strange man at the door says his car has broken down and asks to use the phone. You offer to make the call for him, but he becomes insistent, demanding to be let in. What should you do?
2. Imagine that you are home baby-sitting for your two-year-old sister, Katie. While you are watching TV, she gets into the medicine cabinet and opens a bottle of aspirin. By the time you discover what she has done, the aspirin tablets are scattered everywhere. You can't tell if she has taken any. What should you do? Whom should you call? What should you say?
3. Make a list of the following phone numbers for your wallet:

   - Your parents at work
   - A neighbor
   - The police
   - The fire department
   - The local poison control center.

Reporting Crime

Law enforcement agencies learn about crime through investigation, discovery by police on the street, and crime reports by citizens. Crimes that are not reported cannot be solved. Many crimes are not reported to law enforcement agencies. The U.S. Department of Justice estimates that only half of all crimes are reported. Figure 2 shows which age groups are most likely to report crime.

How to Report a Crime

If you are ever a victim of or a witness to a crime, you should do the following:

- Stay calm. It is very important to report crimes to the police, but sometimes this can be a difficult, trying experience for the victim or witness.
- Call the police immediately!
- Always report a crime. If you don't report it, the police can't help. Someone else may become a victim.
- Tell the police who you are, where you are, and what happened.
- If anyone is hurt, ask for an ambulance.
- When the police arrive, tell them exactly what you saw. If possible, write down what you remember.
- Try to describe the scene of the crime. How many suspects were there? Did they say anything? How did they get away? If the crime was a robbery, what was taken?
- Tell the police what the suspect looked like: age, sex, race, height, weight, clothing, facial features. Was the suspect driving

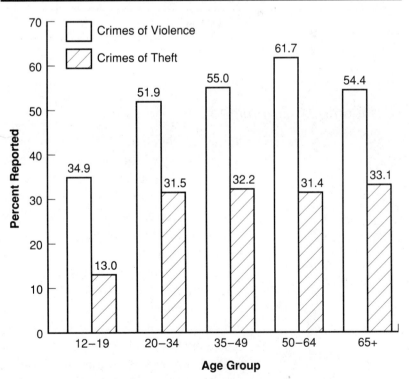

Figure 2–Who reports crime to the police? How teens and adults compare in reporting personal crimes, 1988

Source: U.S. Department of Justice, Bureau of Justice Statistics, *National Crime Survey*, 1988.

a car? If so, try to remember the make, model, color, license number, and which direction it was going when the suspect drove away. If possible, write down the license number.

- You may be asked to make a complaint or to testify in court. Remember, if you don't help the police, the criminal might hurt someone else.
- The police may ask you to attend a lineup or look through photo albums to try to identify the person you saw commit the crime. Do your best.

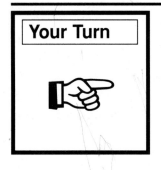

Your Turn

1. According to Figure 2, what age group is least likely to report crime? Why do you think this is the case? What can be done to encourage people to report violent crimes?
2. What would happen if more teens reported crimes to the police?
3. Are you a good witness? Test your observation skills. Look at a picture for 15 seconds, then turn it over. Have a classmate quiz you about the picture, then list everything you can remember about it. Look at the picture again and decide if you are a good witness.

If a Crime Is Committed . . .

Statistics show that physical resistance increases the risk of serious injury to the victim. A crime victim may choose to resist the offender by attacking the person, running away, or screaming. When a weapon is involved, victims sometimes go along with the crime because of the increased potential for danger to their lives. There is no single reaction or set of reactions that is appropriate in every situation. Victims must trust their instincts.

To stop crimes in progress, police set up certain patrolling patterns. They use plainclothes officers to obtain information about where crime may occur. Clearly these tactics are not the entire answer to preventing or stopping a crime because the police cannot be everywhere at once.

Promptly reporting a crime usually increases the opportunity for the police to apprehend (or catch) the criminal. Victims and witnesses should always report a crime immediately.

Reducing Opportunities for Crime

Many people who commit crimes may do so, at least in part, because they believe they won't get caught or because of an easy opportunity. You can reduce opportunities for crime by taking such measures as locking doors and windows, marking valuable objects with your driver's license number, having neighbors watch your home while you're away, and organizing a Neighborhood or Block Watch in your community. Protect yourself by walking in well-lit areas, walking with friends, not picking up hitchhikers, and knowing what to do if you are being followed.

These tactics can work! For example, when citizens lock their cars, the number of vehicle thefts declines. But even when these kinds of measures were utilized in some parts of the country in the 1960s and 1970s, crime continued to increase. In some instances, criminals simply took their activity to less protected places.

Holding the Offender Accountable

Most crime is committed by a relatively small number of offenders. One crime prevention strategy is to hold offenders more accountable for their actions by incarcerating (jailing) criminals for longer periods of time. Another strategy is **restitution**, which makes the offender take responsibility for the damage resulting from the crime.

In recent years, growing concern for crime victims has led to longer jail sentences. The number of mandatory minimum sentences has increased. Career-criminal laws have been enacted to penalize repeat offenders. Some people oppose increasing sentences, claiming that this will not prevent crime. Others say that even if the person is not rehabilitated, at least he or she is off the street for a longer time.

Longer incarceration is an expensive solution. It costs between $20,000 and $40,000 per year to keep one prisoner in jail. Most state prisons are already overcrowded, and taxpayers in some places may not be willing to pay for more prisons.

Restitution is a less expensive alternative that has come into increasing use. Through restitution, the offender repays the victim for what he or she has stolen or destroyed. If the "victim" is the government or a school (for example, in the case of vandalism), the offender can be made to pay back through community service. In some cases the victim and offender meet to discuss the crime so that the offender can learn how the crime has affected the victim's life. This promotes an understanding that would be almost impossible to obtain through the regular court process.

Attacking Social Ills

If social problems cause crime, as one theory suggests, then one way to prevent crime is to cure the social problems. This type of crime prevention can include such programs as job training and placement, antipoverty programs, family counseling, and the like. This strategy may hold some hope, but it may also be beyond the means of many communities and neighborhoods.

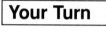

1. Why might two neighborhoods have different crime rates?
2. What are some activities that citizen groups can undertake to prevent crime? Which ones do you think are most likely to work? Why?
3. What are some methods that the police and other government agencies are most likely to use to prevent crime?
4. What crime prevention methods are used in your community?

| **Looking Back** | There is a special section at the back of this book called "Designing a Project." This section provides assistance for teens who decide to participate in community crime prevention projects. Take a look at this section. |

To prepare for a crime prevention project, you need to know more about your community. The following map project will help you gather information on crime and available services in your community. As you gather this information, you may develop some ideas for a specific crime prevention project. Follow these steps:

- Get a large map of your community, organized by political subdivision or police precincts (available from the city planning department or from city hall). This will be your base map.
- Crime statistics for your community should be plotted on your base map. If possible, you should try to get some teenage crime statistics to plot on the map. Use your map to try to find the safest areas of the city.

- You should also plot services on your base map. Where are the following programs and services located?
  - Victim/witness programs
  - Mental health programs
  - Rape crisis centers
  - Counseling centers
  - Women's shelters
- Plot the location of any crime prevention programs on your base map.

What kind of project might you consider designing for your community? Write a brief description of your project idea.

Mapping crime statistics, crime prevention programs, and victim assistance services will help you see your community's crime prevention needs. Once you understand these needs, you and your classmates can design a project to help make the community safer.

2

Victims
of Crime

Words to Know

burglary
robbery
homicide
lobby
advocacy
compensation
amendment

Objectives

As a result of this chapter you should be able to:

■ Identify who are commonly the victims of crime

■ Explain the problems victims face

■ Identify important services for victims

Use Your Experience	Do you know anyone who has been the victim of crime? How did the crime affect the victim? How has the crime affected your school? Your community?

Who Are Victims?

Who are victims of crime in America? Do they make up a very small or very large part of our population? Who is the typical victim? Are victims generally young or old? Poor or rich? Male or female? Following are some statements about crime victims in the United States. Are they true or false?

1. Most Americans will never be victimized by crime.
True or False?

Studies show that sooner or later almost everyone will be touched by crime. In 1988, one in three households was touched by a crime of violence or theft. Each year, over 36 million Americans are victimized at home, at school, or on the street.

2. The age group "65 plus" is most often hit by crime.
True or False?

Believe it or not, older people are victims of crime less often than teens. For all major types of crime, people ages 12 to 19 are the most frequent victims; those 65 and over, the least. Yet the fear of crime is reversed. This makes sense: A teen who is knocked down may be scared and suffer from hurt pride, but the same push can also break an older person's arm or hip.

3. Women are more likely to be victimized than men.
True or False?

Males are twice as likely as females to be victims of crime. Male teenagers are much more likely to be victims than female teens. Nearly half the violent crimes against teens are committed by people they know.

4. The rich are more likely to be victims of crime than the poor.
True or False?

Once again the statement is false. The poor, along with the unemployed and the separated or divorced, are more likely to be crime victims. Even among businesses, it is the owner of a small business, the retailer, who is the hardest hit by crime. **Burglary**, **robbery**, shoplifting, and internal theft add to costs and eat away profits, particularly for small businesses.

5. *Members of minority groups are more likely to be victimized by violent crime. True or False?*

This statement is true. Studies show that African Americans, Hispanics, and other minorities are more likely to be victimized than whites are. Whatever their ethnicity, people are more likely to be victimized by persons of the same ethnic group.

6. *Once people become victims, not much can be done to help them. True or False?*

This is false. Many communities have established victim assistance programs. These programs include rape crisis centers and other counseling programs, drug hot lines, and assistance for victims who go to court.

Your Turn

1. Which of the preceding answers surprised you the most? Why?
2. What feelings do victims of crime have? Are the feelings different depending on the type of crime? If so, how?
3. Why do you think the elderly are fearful of crime? Is this fear justified?
4. Why do you think the poor and minorities are more likely to be victims of crime?

Facts About Crime Victims

- The most typical crime victim is a male teenager who is African American or Hispanic, unmarried, and poor or unemployed.
- The younger the person (down to age 16), the more likely he or she is to be a victim. Younger teens (ages 12 to 15) are also victims far more often than adults are. The full extent to which children under 12 are victims is not known because it is almost impossible to design surveys to measure these crimes.
- Americans have a one in 10,000 chance of being murdered in any given year, but a one in 133 chance over a lifetime. African American males have the highest probability of being murdered—a one in 21 lifetime risk.
- Students and the unemployed are more likely than homemakers, retirees, or the employed to be victims of crime.
- If a person looks vulnerable, it adds to the risk of victimization. Persons who are physically disabled or who appear feeble,

depressed, or mentally incompetent are more likely than the general population to be victims of crime.

- According to the 1988 *National Crime Survey*, 58 percent of violent crimes were committed by people who were strangers to the victims; 42 percent were committed by a victim's acquaintance or relative.

- When the victims and the assailant know one another, the victim's chances of being injured are higher. But when the victim knows the assailant, it is also less likely that the crime will be reported.

- According to the 1988 *National Crime Survey*, except for rape, Hispanics are somewhat more likely than non-Hispanics to be victims of violent crimes (34.9 per 1,000 compared with 29.3 per 1,000).

Repairing damage done to property is one way teens can help crime victims.

In Your Community

Contact your local police department, state attorney general's office, or department of public safety to find out the following information:

1. How many **homicides** (murders) occurred in your community in the past year?
2. How many rapes, robberies, burglaries, and auto thefts occurred in your community during the past year?
3. Is the crime rate in your neighborhood going up or down? Do some neighborhoods have more crime than others? Which ones? Why?

The Costs of Crime

For most victims, the economic cost of crime is moderate to serious, but for some it is devastating. Most crimes are property crimes, in which criminals take the money or property of others. Violent crime also causes financial loss and expense (lost income, for example), as do vandalism and other crimes without economic motives.

A 1980 study showed that the poor suffered much greater losses from crime than those with high incomes.

Crime frequently results in medical expenses—sometimes enormous ones. Most assaults do not produce major physical injuries. But a number do cause severe injury that results in high medical care costs. For victims who are paralyzed, disfigured, or otherwise permanently injured, the medical costs of the crime may never end.

Crime exacts emotional costs that can be severe and long lasting. They are in many cases the most significant harm victims endure.

Initial feelings of shock often give way in time to overwhelming feelings of fear or anger. These feelings can last for days or even months. But an even more surprising reaction is the victim's sense of guilt. Victims often blame themselves rather than the criminal: "It was my fault" or "I was stupid," they think.

A special source of distress for almost half the victims of criminal violence is that their assaulters are people they know. Many of these assailants are close friends or family members who betrayed the victim's trust in them.

Many victims, struggling to regain control, are freshly pained when others—who mean well—continue to make decisions that exert control over their lives or that resurrect the crime experience. Friends and family members can open the wounds even without directly suggesting the victim is at fault (by asking questions like "What were you doing out so late at night?").

Teens who get hurt while taking risks often have a rough time afterward. They get the message that they were in the wrong place at the wrong time. But they don't get other messages, such as "I'm glad you're safe" or "No one had a right to hurt you, even if you were taking chances."

Friends and family may send subtle messages that victims should have done more. Or they may withdraw from the victim, unsure of what to say or do. Old friends may shun surviving family members after a murder, for instance. Even loving relatives and friends may become impatient when victims take a long time to get over their trauma.

Sometimes the court process upsets victims. Though many states have enacted new laws, victims for years were expected to take time off from work without any compensation in order to attend the trial. They also paid for their own transportation, meals, child care, and other expenses.

A nationwide "victims movement" has coordinated and reinforced local efforts and drawn national attention to wrongs against victims and ways to right them. Increasingly, champions of this movement are former victims themselves, like the founders of Mothers Against Drunk Driving, Parents of Murdered Children, Victims for Victims, and other groups. One example of a victim who has become an activist is Betty Jane Spencer.

In Your Community

1. What are the costs of crime in your community? Are they all financial?
2. Do the costs affect the way of life in your neighborhood?

The Case of Betty Jane Spencer

On the night of February 14, 1977, Betty Jane Spencer and her sons Ralph, age 14, Reeve, 16, Raymond, 18, and Greg, 22, were at their home in a rural county in southwest Indiana. Betty's husband Keith was at work at a local television station.

When the family heard someone outside, they opened the front door and were confronted by four young men, ages 17, 20, 21, and 23. These men, all armed with guns, forced their way in and ransacked the house looking for things to steal. After 30 minutes or so, the intruders ordered Betty and her sons to lie face down on the living room carpet and shot them all. The four boys were murdered. Somehow, despite having been shot three times in the back and shoulder, Betty managed to get to a neighbor's house to call for help. Betty's injuries were so serious that it took her months to recuperate. As she would later say, "They murdered all five of us that night. I just happened to survive."

The crime disrupted the normally calm atmosphere of this community, where people didn't even lock their doors. The boys' friends and the friends' parents grieved, and many suddenly felt vulnerable themselves. In the first few months after the murders, some 800 new gun permits were issued to county residents who were concerned about their safety and the safety of their families. The trusting and open atmosphere of the community gave way to anxiety and fear.

The police began their investigation by noting Betty's description of the four young men. Because the police were so concerned about the couple's safety, Betty and Keith were not allowed to return to their house right away. It was not until a month later that a tip from a police informant paid off, and the first of the four suspects was arrested. Within a few months, all four had been apprehended and two had confessed.

The trials for the two suspects who did not confess were held in the next county because of all the publicity. Betty's testimony recounting the agonizing events of that February night was a significant help to prosecutors. All four men are in prison today serving life sentences.

In the years after the murder, Betty and Keith worked at ways of dealing with their grief over the loss of their sons. In 1979, Betty joined Protect the Innocent (PTI), an Indiana group that works to strengthen the state's criminal laws and the rights of victims.

Along with other victims of crime who had joined PTI, Betty successfully **lobbied** the Indiana legislature for the passage of several laws. The new laws focused on tightening bail and parole procedures, providing standards for a "guilty but mentally ill" defense, and requiring judicial review of proposed releases of criminally insane patients from state hospitals.

In addition to her work with PTI, Betty trained to become a crisis counselor who works with individual victims. Volunteer work helped her recover emotionally, she says "but recovery is never complete after a thing like that. The thing that you work for is to have more good days than bad ones. For me, becoming an activist helped me get there. It gave some meaning to my boys' death if I could make it a little easier for other victims."

In 1988, Betty and Keith separated, and she moved to Florida. "Family members who have been traumatized by violent crime come out of their ordeal very different people. We see a high level of estrangement and divorce in victimized families," Betty explained, adding, "Unfortunately, Keith and I had to pay that hidden cost of crime."

Betty is now the director of the Florida state office of Mothers Against Drunk Driving (MADD) and is continuing her lobbying and victim assistance work through that organization.

Your Turn

1. Who was Betty Jane Spencer? What happened to her?
2. Do you think her experience as a victim was typical or unusual? Explain your answer.
3. What did she do after she began to recover from the crime? What types of issues did she work on?
4. Why do you think it helped Betty to share her experience with other victims?

How Does Crime Affect Its Victims?

Crime has three obvious effects on victims—and several less obvious ones. Victims go through a difficult experience even if the crime was a property crime (like burglary) rather than a violent personal crime.

Psychologists have identified three stages that most victims experience in response to a crime. During the first stage, the victim is often numb, unable to believe that the crime is happening or has just happened. As the victim begins to grasp what has happened, he or she enters the second stage and starts to build up emotional defenses. At this stage, anger, fear, and guilt are typical responses.

During this stage, many victims experience intense feelings that hit them out of the blue for days or weeks on end. Some victims keep reliving the crime in their minds and feel almost

When victims of crime begin to grasp what has happened to them, they commonly experience anger, fear, and guilt.

uncontrollable terror or rage. Still, they can't stop themselves from thinking about it. The intensity of these feelings can be scary: First, the offender took control from the victim, and now the victim's feelings are doing the same thing, making it hard for the victim to concentrate or to enjoy things.

As time passes, the victim comes to terms with the emotional reactions to the crime and begins to focus more on day-to-day living. During this third stage, the problems the crime caused may not have gone away entirely, but the victim is better able to cope with them and is less driven by anger and fear. A person at this stage thinks, "Now I am a former victim—a survivor—and I am in control of my life again."

There is no way to tell how long someone will take to recover from a crime. Often people can be helped by the support and care of others around them. This help, coupled with the assistance of community resources, can make an important difference to a crime victim.

Advocacy for Victims

Victim **advocacy** groups want to ease the effects of crime on victims. These groups feel there is a real need to assert victims' rights within the criminal justice process.

Many of the new programs to help victims are aimed at victims of specific crimes, like rape, spouse abuse, drunk driving, and child abuse. Most of them offer crisis intervention services to the victim as soon after the crime as possible. Some that work closely with police departments send a victim advocate to be with the victim as soon as the responding patrol officer completes an initial report. That advocate will typically work with the victim and the victim's loved ones for several days or weeks, helping them to deal with the practical and emotional consequences of the crime.

When there is an arrest and prosecution, some communities have another advocate who works in the prosecutor's victim/witness program to help ease the victim's participation in the court system, which victims may find overpowering and even frightening.

A third kind of assistance now offered is victim **compensation**, which helps pay for medical expenses, lost wages, and funeral expenses in case of death.

By 1991, there were over 7,800 victim service programs in the United States. Forty-eight states had active victim compensation programs. And between 1980 and 1991, 48 states enacted some form of "crime victims' bill of rights." These laws offer new protections for victims—guaranteeing, for example, that they be given court waiting rooms away from defendants or that they be consulted before the prosecutor enters a plea bargain or reduces charges. Many of these laws were inspired by a list of rights published by the National Organization for Victim Assistance (NOVA) in 1980:

1. Victims and witnesses have a right to be treated with dignity and compassion.
2. Victims and witnesses have a right to protection from intimidation and harm.
3. Victims and witnesses have a right to be informed about the criminal justice process.
4. Victims and witnesses have a right to counsel.

5. Victims and witnesses have a right to receive compensation for damages.
6. Victims and witnesses have a right to preservation of property and employment.
7. Victims and witnesses have a right to due process in criminal court proceedings.

Some of the state laws on victims' rights do not give victims a way to appeal to a court for help if they believe their rights have been violated or not protected. Many victim advocates believe that the absence of this ability to appeal and the failure of some states to enforce victims' rights have left victims without the protection that the law is supposed to provide. To protect these rights and to be sure that violations are addressed, some victims have lobbied for a victims' rights **amendment** to their state constitution. Such amendments give victims the ability to get court orders that will enforce their rights. Many of the amendments also reaffirm what is already in the state law about the victim's right to be present at or informed of all court proceedings.

As of January, 1991, six states, including Arizona (1990), Florida (1988), Michigan (1988), Rhode Island (1986), Texas (1989) and Washington (1989), had adopted constitutional amendments on victims' rights. An additional dozen states were considering similar amendments.

Your Turn

1. If you were the victim of a robbery, what concerns would be most important to you? How would your feelings differ if the crime were vandalism?
2. Do the police or the courts ever add to the problems of victims? In what ways can police help victims? In what ways can the legal system help victims?

Victim/Witness Assistance and Crime Prevention

It is the victim or witness who comes forth to report a crime and testify in court. Making it less intimidating and easier for victims and witnesses to report and testify helps prevent crime because it improves the chances that the criminal will be caught.

Victim assistance can be an important part of any community crime prevention effort. Neighbors can provide urgently needed help when crime has struck.

Victim services are a very important part of community crime prevention.

Teaching a victim how to prevent further crimes can help restore the victim's sense of control and ease fears. At the same time, one must use common sense to avoid suggesting that the victim should have somehow prevented the crime in the first place.

In Your Community

1. Does your state have a victim compensation program? If so, who is eligible and for what benefits?
2. Does your state have a victims' bill of rights? If so, what are its provisions?
3. Which of the following services are established in your community: a rape crisis center, a battered women's shelter, a crisis intervention program for victims of other crimes, a court or prosecutor's victim/witness program? Are there other victim service programs in your community?
4. Is there a victims' rights amendment to your state constitution? What does it say?

What Can You Do?

- Help your local crime prevention group alert members to victims' needs.
- Develop a directory of community resources that help victims.
- Help a neighbor who has been a victim. Listen, or help with errands, child care, or other tasks. Know what further assistance is available.
- Go to court as supportive company with a neighbor who has been victimized.
- Investigate and seek to upgrade victim compensation and victims' rights laws in your state.

A number of national, state, and local organizations can provide more information about victim rights and services. Three national sources are:

- National Organization for Victim Assistance (NOVA)
  1757 Park Road, NW
  Washington, D.C. 20010
  (202) 232-6682

- National Victim Resource Center
  Office for Victims of Crime
  U.S. Department of Justice
  633 Indiana Avenue, NW
  Washington, D.C. 20531
  (202) 724-6134

- National Victim Center
  307 West 7th Street, Suite 1001
  Fort Worth, TX 76102
  (817) 877-3355

If a Friend Is Hit by Crime . . .

There are a number of things you can do to help a friend who's been victimized by crime. Some are practical steps to make the victim's life a bit easier; others are emotional support steps to help the victim recover as quickly as he or she can. Don't assume that a male friend will handle being a victim better than a female friend. Any friend needs support.

1. Just be there. Let your friend know you care and that you will be glad to listen or talk—whether it's about the crime or some other subject. Your friend may want to retell the entire incident one day but recoil from even mentioning it the next.

Understand that this is normal, especially in the early stages of recovery.

2. Let your friend know you are sorry the crime happened and that you blame the criminal, not your friend, for the crime.

3. Avoid telling the victim you "understand" or "know" how it feels even if you've been a victim of the same or a similar crime yourself. We all tend to hurt in different ways.

4. Be prepared for your friend to have confused and intense emotions about the event and about his or her treatment by police, hospital personnel, and others.

5. Help with day-to-day chores your friend may not be ready to cope with—preparing meals, watching children, keeping up with school assignments, making minor household repairs.

6. Know what resources—victim counseling hot lines, and so forth—could help your friend. Emphasize that it's natural to seek trained help in dealing with crime, which is a violent trauma to anyone.

Just being there for a friend who has been the victim of a crime can be very important.

Your Turn

Your friend Martha is mugged on the way home from school. She is in the hospital with a broken arm and a concussion.

1. What do you think her feelings are? What issues will she have to deal with because of this crime?
2. What kinds of problems could she have in the future?
3. What could you do to help with her practical problems? With her emotional problems?
4. Who else might be hurt or troubled because of the crime against Martha?

Looking Back

Assume you are a scriptwriter at a local radio station. You have been asked to draft a public service announcement directed at teenagers about preventing teen victimization or providing help for teens who have been victims of crimes. Write an announcement that will be effective in getting your message across to teens.

3

Violent Crime

Words to Know

homicide
rape
robbery
assault
aggravated assault
simple assault
gangs

Objectives

As a result of this chapter you should be able to:

- Define violent crime

- Discuss the characteristics of the most serious violent crimes

- Identify strategies for preventing and avoiding violent crime

- Discuss the role drugs play in the increase in violent crime

| **Use Your Experience** | What crimes do you think of as being "violent?" Do you know anyone who has been the victim of a violent crime? How does violent crime affect individuals? How does it affect your community? |

What Is Violent Crime?

Violent crime refers to events such as homicide, rape, and assault that may result in death or bodily injury. Robbery is also considered a violent crime because it involves the use or threat of force against a person.

Homicide is intentionally causing the death of another person. While homicide is committed less frequently than other violent crimes, the United States has more murders per year than almost any other country. Over half of all murderers are known by their victims. Homicide often carries a sentence ranging from thirty years to life in prison, or even the death penalty.

Rape, sometimes referred to as sexual assault, is the crime of forcing a person to submit to sexual intercourse. According to the *National Crime Survey*, approximately 80 percent* of the rapes in 1989 occurred between 6:00 P.M. and 6:00 A.M., and about 27 percent were committed in the victim's home. Males as well as females can be victims of sexual assault. This crime usually carries a penalty of 20 years or more in prison.

Robbery is unlawfully taking or trying to take another person's property by using or threatening the use of force. Robbery often involves more than one offender. Less than half of all robberies involve the use of a weapon.

Figure 1–Violent crimes reported to the police, 1989	Type	Number per 100,000 Population	Percentage of Total Reported Violent Crimes
	Murder	8.7	1.3%
	Forcible rape	38.1	5.7%
	Robbery	233.0	35.2%
	Aggravated assault	383.4	57.8%
	Total	663.2	100%

Source: FBI, *Uniform Crime Reports,* 1989.

*Percentages are estimates from the Bureau of Justice Statistics, U.S. Department of Justice, *National Crime Survey,* 1988.

Assault is the most common violent crime. There are two types: simple and aggravated. **Aggravated assault** is the intentional threat or attempt to inflict bodily injury or death with a deadly or dangerous weapon. **Simple assault** is the intentional threat or attempt to inflict less serious bodily injury without a weapon.

Protecting Yourself from Street Assaults

The single most important defense against street crime is to be alert. Alertness often makes the difference between the victim and the nonvictim.

Street criminals are like other predators. They look for an easy mark. Not the oldest, not the youngest, but the easiest—the person who seems to be wandering around in a fog, someone who can easily be taken off guard.

You can take the following actions to help protect yourself from street crime:

- Avoid dark, deserted streets, parking lots, garages, and out-of-the-way bus or subway stops, particularly at night.
- Walk confidently, showing that you know where you are going. Look around. Be alert to your surroundings.
- Don't take shortcuts through deserted parks, tunnels, parking lots, or alleys.
- If you feel concerned about the area where you are walking, change your route or walk toward a busy area.
- If someone seems to be following you, make an abrupt change of direction. If the person keeps walking in the old direction, no harm is done. But if the stranger turns to follow you, your suspicions are confirmed. Take immediate action to be noticed and to get help. Hurry to a lighted area where there is traffic. Don't be afraid to run or yell for help. Many muggers will take off after the first outcry. Street criminals are usually looking for an easy mark.
- When you go out, take a friend. Most assaults happen to lone victims.
- Let someone—parent, brother or sister, or friend—know where you are going and when you will come back. Call if you're going to be late.
- Know your neighborhood—when the stores and restaurants are open, where the police and fire stations are. If you need them, you probably won't have time to hunt.
- Never hitchhike. Accept rides only from people you know and trust.

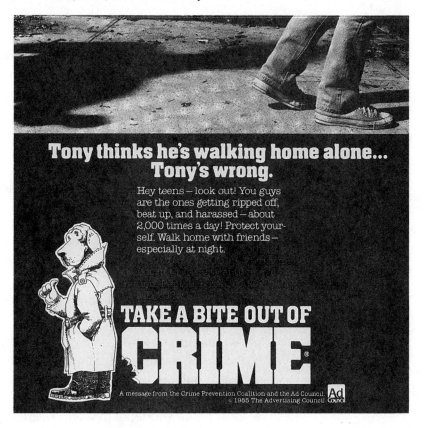

- If you must walk at night, do not walk near cars parked at the curb or close to doorways or shrubbery. Walk in the street if the street isn't too busy.
- If you must walk at night regularly, vary your route. This will minimize the possibility that someone may wait to assault you along the way.
- If a stranger in a car stops to ask directions, remain a good distance from the car to prevent him or her from grabbing you or knocking you down by opening the car door.
- Avoid using drugs or alcohol; they dull your senses, making you more vulnerable under any circumstances.

Your Turn

Role-play a team of police officers giving advice to a group of third-grade students about protecting themselves against street crime. Design a five-minute presentation for the students with the safety information that you feel would be most critical for them to know at their age.

Protecting Yourself from Robbery

The circumstances that result in street assault can also result in robbery. The prevention tips listed for violent crimes can also help prevent robbery. But robbery has some different characteristics and demands some special advice. For example, robbery is more likely to involve multiple offenders against a single victim. A weapon is more likely to be involved.

Look at the following tips for self-protection. What you should do depends upon the situation—how the offender is armed, how many offenders there are, and the location of the crime. These general prevention tips apply to most situations.

Every 19 seconds, a teenager is the victim of a violent crime. You can learn how to reduce your risks of becoming a crime victim. In what ways is this young woman making herself vulnerable to violent crime? How could she reduce her risks of becoming a victim?

Prevent It from Happening in the First Place

- Carry just the money you need that day, but always have enough change for a telephone call.
- Carry your purse or backpack on the side of you farthest from the curb; stay in the middle of the sidewalk.
- If you carry a shoulder-strap purse, it should hang close to your body, protected by your arm.
- Carry handbags with short straps on your arm.
- If followed, don't run straight home unless help is available.
- Try not to carry keys in the same place as your driver's license or other identification as this could tell a robber where those keys fit.
- If you're unsure of or unfamiliar with an area after dark, use taxicabs instead of buses or subways whenever practical.
- When using public restrooms, do not place your backpack or purse on the floor where it can be easily seen and picked up.

Take the Best Course if There Is a Robbery Attempt

- Don't panic. Stay calm.
- If approached by a robber, cooperate—give up your valuables, especially if the criminal has a weapon. It is better to surrender your jacket, even if it means a lot to you, than to be killed or seriously injured.
- Don't make any sudden moves—the offender is probably as nervous as you are.

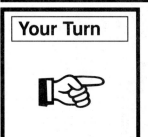

Your Turn

1. What kinds of street crime are a problem in your community?
2. What is the best defense against street crime?
3. If you were walking down the street at night and thought someone was following you, what would you do?
4. If you were walking home from school and some other teens confronted you and tried to rob you, what would you do?

Protect Yourself in Transit

- When using public transportation, sit near the driver or conductor if possible. Take care, however, to avoid the seat nearest an exit door.

- When waiting for a bus, subway, traffic light, or friend, be alert. Your stationary position makes you more vulnerable to attack.

Protect Yourself in Your Car

- Maintain the car as well as possible. Keep the gas tank at least half full.
- Park in well-lighted areas and always lock the car, even if you expect to be gone for only a few minutes.
- Have your keys ready to unlock your car door as you approach the car.
- Before entering the car, check the back seat for someone hiding there.
- Always lock your car doors when you are inside the car.
- If someone menaces you from outside the car, be sure doors are locked and windows are rolled up, blow your horn, and proceed carefully and at a safe speed. Drive away from the attacker, using either forward or reverse.
- If you car is disabled, turn off the engine, put on the flashers, lift the hood, and tie a white cloth around the antenna. Then roll up the windows, and lock yourself in your car. If you have a CB (citizens band) radio or cellular phone, call for help. If someone stops to offer aid, ask him or her through a closed (or slightly cracked) window to telephone for assistance.
- Never pick up hitchhikers.
- Be careful about your keys. Leave only the ignition key with parking or service station attendants.

Protect Yourself in Your Home

- Have your keys ready so that you can unlock the door and enter your residence quickly.
- If you arrive home and think an intruder may be inside, do not enter. Go to a neighbor's house and call the police.
- If no one else is home, check before entering for signs of break-in (indicated by broken windows, open doors, and so on).
- Curtains, blinds, or shades should be used on windows to provide privacy.
- Outside doors should have strong, one-inch-throw dead-bolt locks.
- Illuminate or eliminate places an intruder might be concealed—trees, shrubbery, stairwells, alleys, hallways, and entryways.

- Never open the door until the caller has clearly identified himself or herself, and you have checked out that identity. Do not allow anyone into your home if you are not comfortable with that person's presence.
- Offer to phone for necessary assistance for any stranger who appears at the door. Do not let the person into your home.
- Be sure all ground-level windows and sliding glass (or similar) doors are securely fastened by a lock that can't be easily burglarized.
- Don't hide keys near the house. Burglars know and will check all the hiding places.

If a Burglar Comes. . .

If you are in your home when you hear an intruder, most authorities suggest you avoid confrontation. Leave and call the police if you can do so safely. Even pretend that you're asleep. As soon as the

A good friend of yours has asked you to help with a problem. Your friend's grandmother lives by herself and she would like some help checking out the safety of her new apartment. Make a list of the six most important areas that you and your friend would want to check. What additional information about safety would you like to discuss with your friend's grandmother?

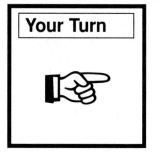

1. *The Dark Street:* The street is dark, so you almost don't spot the three young men leaning against a parked car midway along the block. When you left the party, your friend suggested you walk up Elm Street to First Avenue to get a cab. Now you wonder. As you approach, one of the three youths strolls on ahead of you. The other two silently begin to tag along behind you. Are you about to be held up? Is your fear justified? What should you do?
2. *Someone in Your Home:* When you arrive home, the front door is ajar and the lock seems broken. You know your mom is at work and your dad is out of town on business, so what's going on? You slowly push open the door and hear a noise like someone is ransacking the house. What should you do?

intruder is gone, call the police. Most burglars just want to get in and out quickly. They don't want to turn a property crime into a violent confrontation.

Preventing Rape

Rape is not caused by how someone dresses or looks. It is a power-driven crime in which the attacker seeks to control the victim. Many of the street-, transit-, and car-related tips listed in the previous section can help reduce your risk of being victimized by rape as well as robbery.

Authorities emphasize that 99 out of 100 rapes involve a lone victim. Only a tiny number involve two or more victims. So going places with a trusted friend makes good sense. Three out of five rapes are committed by someone known—at least casually—to the victim, so you should trust your instincts about avoiding potentially hazardous situations even if you think you know the person.

If Someone Tries to Rape You

There are a number of different responses to being attacked. There is no one "best" response. The best choice will depend on where you are, who the attacker is, and your confidence in your own ability to carry out the chosen action. Here are some choices to think about:

- Try not to panic. Look at your attacker, if you are able to, so you can give a description to police. Try to remember things like age, height, weight, build, scars, complexion, and hair color.
- Try stalling for time, distracting the attacker, screaming to attract attention, or fighting back. You may be able to discourage an attack by acting crazy or disgusting. Your best reaction depends on the circumstances and the type of person you are. Trust your instincts.
- If a weapon is used and you feel any response will increase the danger to your life, trust your judgment and submit. The most important thing is that you live through the attack.

If You Are the Victim of Rape

- Get help immediately after the attacker leaves or you get away. Go to a safe place and call the police. Call your parents or someone else close to you.

- Don't bathe, change clothes, douche, or otherwise clean up, whether the rapist succeeded or not. It's natural to want to clean yourself up, but you may wash away or throw away vital evidence.
- The police should take you to a hospital or clinic for an examination to secure evidence to help prosecute your attacker. You may be tested for sexually transmitted diseases. Take a change of clothing when you go to the hospital because your clothes may be needed for evidence.
- Arrange an additional checkup with your own doctor for disease and pregnancy detection.
- As soon as you can, write down or tape-record everything you recall about the incident and about the time immediately before and after it. Do this in several sessions because you may not remember everything the first time.
- You may feel anger, hopelessness, terror, guilt, and helplessness. Get help to deal with these feelings. They are entirely normal after your experience, but they deserve professional attention.
- Get in touch with the nearest rape crisis center or hot line. The police or hospital personnel may have the phone number. Otherwise, these centers are usually listed in the phone book.

You are a girl on your first date with Freddy. You don't know much about him, but he seemed nice enough until he stopped the car on a deserted road near City Park. "Don't be so uptight," he says. "If you didn't want to have sex with me, why are you here?" What should you do?

1. What can public transit authorities do to make passengers in your community safer?
2. Suppose there have been several rapes in the area of the city where your school is located. What would you do to reduce fear on the part of students at your school? To increase the safety of your classmates?

Assault: The Most Common Violent Crime

Assault is the most common violent crime. It is five times more likely than robbery to happen to someone 12 to 19 years of age.

Assaults can range from verbal threats to injuries so severe the victim is near death. The U.S. Bureau of Justice Statistics defines two main categories: aggravated assault and simple assault.

Aggravated assault involves attack with a weapon (no actual injury is required). It also involves attack without a weapon resulting either in serious injury (for example, broken bones, loss of teeth, internal injuries, loss of consciousness) or in any injury requiring two or more days of hospitalization. This includes attempted assault with a weapon. Often this crime carries a penalty of five years or more in prison.

Simple assault involves attack without a weapon, resulting either in minor injury (for example, bruises, black eyes, cuts, scratches, swelling) or in any injury requiring fewer than two days of hospitalization. This includes attempted assault without a weapon. This crime often carries a penalty of six months or more in jail.

Strangers account for slightly more than 4 of every 10 assaults of 12- to 19-year-olds and for roughly half of all aggravated assaults.

Two-thirds of assaults on teens are committed by other teens, whether they are strangers or nonstrangers to the victim. As you may have gathered, assaults can include fights, bullying, and other confrontations, even between friends. Assaults can take place in schools, on the street, in a parking lot, in a park, or in your own home or yard. Weapons used in aggravated assault can range from a knife to a gun, rock, or tree limb.

Figure 2–Teen victims of assault (per thousand persons in age group)

Type	Ages 12–15	Ages 16–19
All assaults	49.4	58.8
Aggravated assaults	14.9	22.1
Completed with injury	4.7	8.9
Attempted with weapon	10.2	13.2
Simple assaults	34.4	36.7
Completed with injury	9.1	11.7
Attempted without weapon	25.4	25.0

Source: U.S. Department of Justice, Bureau of Justice Statistics, *National Crime Survey,* 1988.

Your Turn

1. Do you know someone who has been assaulted? Was it an aggravated or a simple assault?
2. List some situations that could result in an assault either by someone you know or by a stranger. Discuss some ways these assaults could be prevented.

Preventing Assault

There are two major ways you can reduce your chances of being assaulted: Avoid places and situations that could favor this crime and steer clear of people who are violent or uncontrollable.

Many of the basic crime prevention, "street-smart" tips already mentioned—such as not going places alone and avoiding deserted areas or dark shortcuts—can help you reduce your risk of being assaulted. Common-sense rules like not wandering off into unfamiliar territory alone, walking with confidence and self-assurance, staying alert to your surroundings, and crossing the street to avoid potential trouble are good ways to reduce the likelihood that you will be assaulted. Steering clear of assault situations can mean staying away from places where people use drugs or alcohol (some people are more likely to fight if "under the influence"), avoiding confrontations with people known to make a habit of violence, or using common-sense strategies to settle disagreements without violence.

One of the best ways to prevent assaults is to learn how to handle conflict. When you are having a conflict with someone else, be sure to listen carefully to what they say and ask questions to make sure that you understand what is really making them angry. Try to think of as many nonviolent ways to solve the problem as you can. Sometimes people fight because they cannot think of anything else to do. Chapter 6 describes ways to handle conflict nonviolently.

Your Turn

1. Who commits most assaults on teens? Why does this happen?
2. How could you and your friends help each other reduce your chances of being assaulted at school, at home, and in other locations?

In Your Community

Many teens around the country have identified fighting as a problem that they would like to solve at their schools. What types of programs or activities could help solve the problem of fighting at a school? If it were up to you and your classmates to deal with this problem, what type of program would you develop?

Drugs and Violent Crime

There has been a growing public awareness of the linkage between drug abuse and other crime. People who abuse drugs are often involved in crimes, such as robberies and burglaries, to raise money to buy more drugs. Frequently drug use releases inhibitions, making a person less responsible. It can lead to violent outbursts that result in assaults or even murder. Sellers of drugs are known to resort to violence (beatings and killings) to protect their territories or collect money.

Various studies support the association between drugs and violent crime. Following are some of their findings:

- A study of prison inmates revealed that one-third of offenders who committed violent crimes admitted they were under the influence of drugs at the time of their offense, and many had a long history of drug abuse.
- In 22 major cities, at least half (and as many as 82 percent) of those arrested for nondrug-related crimes tested positive for drugs in a 1989 study.
- Drug abusers commit up to three times more crime during periods of active addiction than when they are not using drugs.
- When drug abuse by individuals increases, so does the number and severity of their crimes.
- The likelihood of becoming a crime victim significantly increases with the use of alcohol or other drugs. For example, one study of murder victims found that over 50 percent had alcohol or other drugs in their systems at the time of death.

Two main approaches have emerged in the effort to stop the use and distribution of drugs in the United States. One approach emphasizes ways to reduce the demand for drugs. This approach suggests that we educate people so that they understand the dangers of drugs and can resist the urge to use them. People who favor this point of view feel that the money spent on solving the drug problem should be used for this kind of education and for the rehabilitation of users. These people feel that the problem will never really go away until the demand for drugs is reduced.

On the other hand, many people feel that the continuing supply of illegal drugs to this country prevents us from solving the problem. In their view, the easy availability of drugs entices users, thus creating an illegal market that becomes difficult or impossible to eliminate. Those who hold this view believe that money spent on the drug problem should be used to prevent drugs from reaching the market and to apprehend and punish those who make drugs available. The more effective these measures are, the more likely that the supply of drugs will be reduced, resulting in fewer drug abusers, they say.

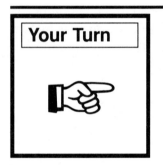

Your Turn

1. Which approach do you feel your community has taken? Has it been effective?
2. What approach do you feel makes the most sense? Write a paragraph explaining the kind of approach you think would be most effective and why.

Gangs and Violent Crime

In common usage, the word **gang** means group or crowd. However, it takes on a different meaning when used in the area of crime and crime prevention. Experts who study gangs describe them as distinct bands of people (generally adolescents and young adults) who see themselves as a group and are involved in shared activities, many of which are violent and illegal. The expression *gang-related* has recently been heard more and more often in discussions of violent and drug-related crime in our society.

Gangs are not limited to large urban areas. Many smaller cities as well as suburban and rural areas are starting to see the signs of gang activity. Graffiti is sometimes the first clue that gangs have formed. Graffiti is used to stake out territory, issue threats, and identify gang involvement in the community. More highly organized gangs may use colors and symbols and may operate according to special group rules.

Some parts of the country have reported increases in gang activity. Much of the increase is due to gang involvement in drug trafficking. The high level of violence connected with this illegal activity is dangerous to the participants and to their communities. Gangs have established elaborate networks of juveniles to work as drug runners to distribute drugs and to assist in the possession, sale, and use of drugs. Older gang members recruit juveniles as workers with the hope of protecting themselves from arrest.

Many of these juveniles become victims of crimes such as assault and homicide because of the role they play in the drug trade. Frequently, innocent bystanders are also victims of drug-related gang violence.

Some experts feel that people join gangs because they need to belong to a peer group that shares common interests and that invites them to participate in activities. The "need to belong" can be hard to overcome, especially when you are a teenager with few community ties. Although it can look attractive, belonging to a gang can be dangerous. Whatever the reason for membership in a gang, it can involve you in activities over which you have little control.

By working together, community members can come up with constructive solutions to difficult problems like gangs and drugs.

Many communities are organizing to respond to the growth in gang membership. One response involves a stronger effort by the juvenile justice system to hold teens responsible for their illegal actions. Another response involves community efforts to sponsor recreation and community service programs that offer teens an alternative to gang membership. The goal of these programs is to renew and strengthen teens' ties to their families, schools, and local community organizations.

In Your Community

1. Is there any indication of gang activity in your community? What clues do you have to support your position?
2. What types of activities does your community offer that would help discourage gang membership?

Your Turn

Your friend has been approached to join a gang. Neither of you has ever belonged to one. Your friend is confused about this choice and comes to you for advice. Role-play the conversation in which you are trying to persuade your friend not to join the gang.

Handguns and Violent Crime

Some of the most serious problems with violent crime in the United States are connected with handguns. Handguns extend the distance from which a person can use force or the threat of force, and the injury they inflict is the most serious of any weapon commonly available. They are also powerful and easy to use, making them attractive to criminals.

Facing an offender armed with a gun can be one of the most frightening experiences in life. It is important to remember this fact when helping a person who has been the victim of a crime involving a gun.

Generally, the best advice is not to resist an offender armed with a gun. Statistics show that in 90 percent of offenses involving handguns, the weapon is never fired. Most often, the handgun is used to intimidate the victim. Resisting increases the chance that the victim will be shot and perhaps killed. However, this advice may not apply to every situation.

Although violent crime is very frightening, it is important for people faced with it to try to concentrate on the characteristics of the offender (clothes, build, face, voice, and so on) as well as on those of the gun. Such information is vital to the police in their efforts to arrest the offender. Above all, report the crime as soon as possible.

The following sections provide some key points to remember about handgun-related violent crime.

Being confronted by an offender armed with a gun can be an enormously frightening experience.

Types of Violent Crime

In 1989 more than 400,000 robberies and assaults were committed with a handgun. One out of every 10 violent crimes and one-fourth of all violent crimes committed by an armed offender involved a handgun.

Homicides

Also in 1989, 11,832 victims of homicide (62 percent of the victims) were killed by offenders using firearms, including handguns. For 16- to 19-year-olds, the murder victimization rate of black males is eight times that of white males.

Victims

In the majority of murders, the victim knew the offender. Among surviving crime victims injured by a handgun, one in three is injured seriously.

Youths as Victims

The number of 15- to 19-year-olds who were victims of handgun murder increased by 107 percent from 1984 to 1989. For 10- to 14-year-olds, the increase was 77 percent. Guns have been used in 60 percent of teen suicides in recent years.

Reducing the Use of Handguns in Crime

There are different theories on how to reduce handgun-related crime. Some people suggest concentrating on convincing individuals to change their behavior voluntarily. Others believe laws and regulations are necessary.

Efforts to change people's behavior can include teaching them to handle conflict without violence, trying to convince them not to possess or own a handgun, and teaching the safe and lawful use of handguns.

There has been a lot of debate about proposed laws to limit the types of handguns that can be legally owned or to limit ownership to certain people. People who oppose proposed restrictions say that the Second Amendment to the U.S. Constitution gives all citizens a right to own whatever type of firearm they want. They also point out that the criminals, not the weapons, present the problem to society.

People in favor of restrictions argue that the Second Amendment was meant to allow for the creation of state militia units, not to permit ownership of dangerous weapons like handguns by any citizen. These people believe that restrictions or prohibitions on gun ownership would help to reduce violent crime and thus help citizens feel safer.

Government at all levels has concerned itself with how to reduce crime committed with handguns. Measures already taken by some state or local governments include:

- Bans on particular types of firearms, such as plastic or other small handguns, pistols, or machine guns
- Requirements for a waiting period prior to the issuance of a gun permit, which allows time to check a person's background for criminal activity, drug-abuse, or other related history
- Stiffer sentences for those convicted of crimes committed with firearms
- Restrictions or prohibitions on the concealment of firearms or on their use or possession in heavily populated areas or in vehicles.

Your Turn

Many television programs and movies show people shooting others and using other forms of violence to solve their problems. Do you think that the portrayal of violence on television and in the movies makes people more likely to use violence to solve their own problems? Why or why not? If you feel that television and the movies promote violence, what types of activities could reverse their influence? What other influences might reduce people's tendency to solve problems by using violence?

In Your Community

Find an example of violent crime in your local newspaper. Write a paragraph about the crime. Be sure to include the following information:

- What crime is described in the article?
- Why do you consider it a violent crime?
- What effect do you think this crime had on the victim(s)?
- Was there any way to avoid this crime?
- What types of resources can your community offer the victim(s) of this crime?

**Looking
Back**

You have been appointed by the mayor of your city to sit on the Commission to Prevent Violent Crime. The goal of the commission is to develop a citywide plan to reduce violent crime.

What are the most important issues that should be considered by the commission? How should it collect information about these issues? Draw up three recommendations that the commission could make to reduce violent crime.

4

Property Crime and Vandalism

Words to Know

property crime
robbery
larceny
burglary
auto theft
embezzlement
forgery
defraud
extortion
receiving stolen
    property
fraud
copyright violation
vandalism
arson
environmental
    design
patent
software piracy

Objectives

As a result of this chapter you should be able to:

- Define property crime and apply the definition to specific situations

- Discuss methods teens can use to protect their property

- Describe the nature, causes, and costs of property crime, including vandalism

- Recommend strategies that can be used to protect your property from crimes in school, at home, and in the community

| Use Your Experience | Do you know anyone who has been the victim of vandalism? Do you know anyone whose house has been burglarized or whose car has been stolen? |

What Is Property?

Property is anything that is owned or can be owned, such as land, cars, money, bicycles, televisions, computer programs, and other items. As our society has changed, our ideas about property have expanded. For example, intellectual creations such as written ideas, recipes for brand-name foods, songs, and video games are now also considered property. Just like a car or bicycle, such items can be unlawfully taken.

What Is Property Crime?

A **property crime** occurs when possessions are taken or destroyed illegally without the use or threat of force against the individual. Larceny, forgery, and auto theft are examples. Property crimes that involve destruction include such acts as vandalism, arson, and introducing computer viruses that erase data from computer systems. Sometimes crimes begin as property crimes and turn into violent crimes. For example, you might return to your apartment during a burglary attempt and surprise the burglar. The surprise could result in injury to you.

Robbery is a violent crime that involves the taking of property. Robbery involves the illegal taking of property from the immediate possession of another person by use of force or intimidation. In many states the law imposes stricter penalties for armed robbery.

Which Are More Frequent, Property Crimes or Violent Crimes?

Property crime is the most prevalent type of crime in the United States. Roughly nine out of every ten crimes is a property-related offense.

Property crime victims are frequently psychologically damaged. They feel violated and vulnerable. They have unanswered questions about their safety. Were the criminals watching the house? Are they still watching? What were they looking for? Figure 1 shows a comparison between property crime and violent crime. Figure 2 shows the various percentages of property and violent crimes reported to the police.

Figure 1–Property crimes versus violent crimes, 1989

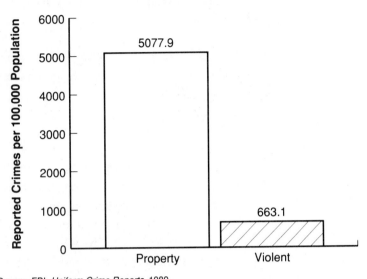

Source: FBI, *Uniform Crime Reports*, 1989.

Types of Property Crime

In general, property crimes can be divided into two major categories:

1. Acts that involve stealing or taking the property of another, such as larceny, burglary, auto theft, embezzlement, forgery, extortion, fraud, and copyright violation
2. Acts that involve destruction of property, such as vandalism and arson.

Larceny is taking or attempting to take property (except motor vehicles) from someone else without permission. Picking someone's pocket, stealing a bicycle or bicycle parts, and stealing items from cars are examples of larceny.

According to statistics on crime published in the *Uniform Crime Reports* by the Federal Bureau of Investigation (FBI), 1,254,220 people were arrested for larcenies in 1989 alone. Of those arrested, 8 percent were under the age of 18. The average amount lost by a larceny victim in 1989 was $462. The amount lost by all larceny victims in 1989 was estimated at $3.6 billion.

Burglary is the unlawful entry into any fixed structure or vehicle used for residential, industrial, or business purposes (with or without force) with the intent to commit a crime.

According to the FBI *Uniform Crime Reports*, there were 3,168,170 burglaries reported to the police in 1989. Two out of three were residential burglaries. Almost 32 percent of the 356,717 people arrested for burglary in 1989 were under the age of 18. The only areas in the country where the rate of burglary increased from 1988 to 1989 were in cities of fewer than 10,000 residents.

The average loss by a victim of burglary in 1989 was $1,060. The total loss by all burglary victims in 1989 was estimated at $3.4 billion.

Auto theft is taking or attempting to take the vehicle of another person without permission. In the case of joyriding, both the driver and the passenger are considered thieves. Car theft is relatively well reported to the police because reporting is required for insurance claims. Over 40 percent of those arrested for auto theft are under 21 years of age.

Embezzlement is the intentional taking of property for personal benefit by someone to whom it was entrusted. Examples of embezzlement include a store clerk's taking money from a cash drawer or taking merchandise without paying. A stockbroker who takes money that should have been invested for someone else is also committing embezzlement.

Forgery is changing a document with the intent to **defraud** (trick). This crime includes signing someone else's name to a check and then cashing it.

Extortion is sometimes called *blackmail*. It involves the use of threats to obtain the property of another. This can include threats of physical harm, property destruction, or injury to someone's reputation.

Receiving stolen property is intentionally accepting property that you know or have reason to believe is stolen. Knowledge that the property is stolen can be implied by the situation. This crime is usually a felony if the property received is valued at more than a certain amount (for example, $100). This amount depends on state law. Receiving stolen property of lesser value is a misdemeanor.

Fraud is obtaining money or other things of value under false pretenses. Fraud usually involves deceiving or tricking the victim into voluntarily giving the offender the valuables.

Copyright violation is the reproduction by any means (including photocopying) of substantial portions of the work of another person or group that is protected under copyright laws.

Vandalism, sometimes referred to as *malicious mischief*, is the willful destruction of the property of another person.

Arson is the intentional destruction of property by means of fire or explosion with or without the consent of the owner. In 1985 annual losses due to arson were estimated at $1.3 billion.

Your Turn

a. Larceny
b. Robbery
c. Forgery
d. Burglary
e. Auto theft
f. Vandalism
g. Arson
h. Embezzlement
i. Extortion
j. Receiving stolen property
k. Not a property crime
l. Shoplifting

Read the following statements. On a separate sheet write the letter of the item that applies beside each statement.

1. Joe sets fire to his warehouse.
2. Ralph signs his mother's name to a check he has taken from her checkbook and cashes it.
3. The bank teller deposits $1 in her bank account from every customer deposit made at her window.
4. Arnold uses a knife to persuade James to give up his watch.
5. Dionne borrows her neighbor's new car without asking permission.
6. Jose is playing video games at the arcade. Another teen offers Jose the chance to buy a $400 bicycle for only $100. Jose takes him up on the offer.
7. Carl and his friends use firecrackers to blow up mailboxes along country roads.
8. A group of graduating seniors spray-paint "CLASS OF 1995" on the stadium walls.
9. Mary fails her chemistry exam. She feels the exam was unfair. To show the teacher how unfair she thinks the test was, she goes to the chemistry lab during her study period and breaks test tubes, beakers, and other chemistry equipment.
10. Melinda likes to run errands for elderly neighbors in the housing complex where she lives. Sometimes she does not return all the change when she goes to the store for them.
11. Manuel wants to test his school's emergency preparedness. He goes to the lab area, finds a cupboard where cleaning rags are kept, and uses his lighter to set the rags on fire.
12. Alicia leaves her purse in the math classroom while she goes to her locker. When she returns, her purse has been taken.
13. Derrick rents a videotape of a movie. He likes the movie so much he switches the label to a blank tape and keeps the rental tape.
14. Bob rides his dirt bike through a city park. Even though the ground is muddy, he rides in circles on the baseball infield.

How Are Teens Affected by Crimes of Theft?

Each year from 1985 to 1988 in the United States, 3,328,658 teens, or an average of more than one in ten, were victims of a crime of theft. However, that figure does not accurately describe the extent of teen victimization. The *National Crime Survey* of

1988 shows that only 26 percent of thefts from teens that involved items worth more than $50 were reported to the police. Over 80 percent of thefts from 12- to 15-year-olds in 1988 occurred at school. Nearly 40 percent of thefts from 16- to 19-year-olds occurred at school, while 21 percent happened on public transportation or in parking lots.

Figure 2–Property crimes reported to the police in the United States, 1989

Type	Number per 100,000 Population	Percentage of Total Reported Property Crimes
Burglary	1276.3	25.1%
Larceny	3171.3	62.5%
Motor vehicle theft	630.4	12.4%
Total	5077.9	100%

Source: FBI, *Uniform Crime Reports*, 1989.

Your Turn

Use Figure 3 to answer the following questions.

1. What age group is most frequently victimized by theft? Why?
2. What age group has the lowest rate of crimes of theft? Why?

Figure 3–Crime victims by age group and type of crime, 1988

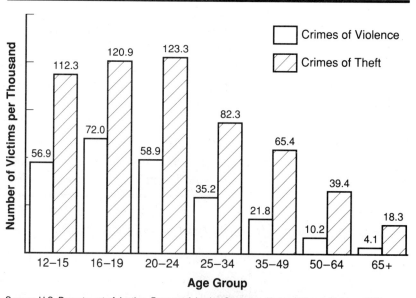

Source: U.S. Department of Justice, Bureau of Justice Statistics, *National Crime Survey*, 1988.

Preventing Theft

At Home

- Be sure outside doors have strong, one-inch-throw dead-bolt locks.
- Use good locks on all first-floor windows.
- Illuminate or eliminate places an intruder might hide: trees, shrubbery, stairwells, alleys, hallways, and entryways.
- Keep a light on when you are not at home.
- Ask a neighbor to watch the house when you are on vacation.
- Mark valuables such as televisions, cameras, typewriters, and stereos with your state and driver's license number.
- Keep your bike and any sports equipment inside the house when not in use.
- Avoid confrontations with burglars.

At School

- Keep your locker locked. Don't keep money or anything valuable in your locker, especially overnight, through the weekend, or over the holidays.
- Lock your bike with a hardened U-shaped lock. Don't leave your bike in an isolated area. Taking a wheel off helps discourage thefts.
- Don't leave your purse, backpack, or other bag unattended.

In Your Car

- Try to park in well-lighted areas.
- Never leave keys in the car.
- Always lock the car, even if it's in your own driveway.
- Never leave the motor running when no one's in the car.
- Mark car stereos, speakers, and CB radios with your driver's license number. If they can be easily disconnected, lock them in your trunk when you leave your car.
- Never leave valuables in plain view when leaving your car, even if it's locked. Put them in the trunk or at least out of sight. When possible, put them in the trunk before you arrive at your destination so people don't see you hiding your valuables.

Out and About

- Don't leave your purse or wallet on the counter while you're looking at something in a store.

- Don't dangle or swing your purse or pack by the straps. Carry it close to you, especially in crowded stores and streets. Keep a wallet in a side or front, not back, pocket.
- Be wary of anybody who tries to sell you something at a price that sounds too good to be true.

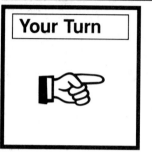

Your Turn

You spent six months saving money from your after-school job so that you could afford to buy a high-quality portable radio and compact disc player. You are proud that you bought it yourself and excited that you don't have to listen to your favorite music on the little kitchen radio anymore. One night, you decide to bring your new prized possession to the park to show it to some friends. While you are playing ball with them, you look over and notice that your radio is gone—someone has stolen it.

What feelings would you have? What would you do about the theft? What would you do if someone told you a person you knew had taken it? What, if anything, do you think you might learn from such an experience?

Organizing Neighborhood Groups to Prevent Property Crime

Organized neighborhood groups whose aim is to prevent crime have been in existence in the United States since the late 1960s. These groups, often called Neighborhood Watch or Block Watch, are organized by residents or existing block associations concerned about crime. The groups, which receive assistance from local law enforcement officials, try to build a safer community by watching out for criminal activity or suspicious behavior, reporting crime, and building closer neighborhood relationships. These groups have been very successful in their efforts to reduce property crime.

Types of activities that all Neighborhood Watch groups get involved in include:

- Home security education—Residents get tips on how to use locks, lighting, fences, and shrubbery to make their homes less attractive to burglars.
- Property marking—Residents are taught to mark valuables with identifying numbers.
- Neighborhood watch—Residents are advised on how to report crimes and suspicious activity to the police.

Sometimes the group conducts activities geared specifically to the needs of its community, such as providing special programs for children or for the elderly who are at home alone.

The following are some examples of Neighborhood Watch success stories:

- An Atlanta block association concerned about crime, abandoned homes and cars, poor street lighting, and vacant lots got residents together to address these issues. The residents turned a vacant lot into a community events site and organized block parties. Because of their efforts, crime and fear of crime have been reduced in that area, and more people are out and about in the neighborhood.

- In one Pennsylvania town, two out of every three people belong to Neighborhood Watch. Since 1985 the community's crime prevention expertise has provided help to the deaf, blind, and physically handicapped as well as to senior citizens. For example, community volunteers periodically visit elderly people who live alone in order to check on safety and to offer to help with day-to-day needs.

- In 1986 a Richmond, Virginia, neighborhood experienced three murders, two rapes, and 134 burglaries. A community volunteer organized and educated residents on crime prevention issues so well that in 1988 there were no murders, no rapes, and only 20 burglaries in that neighborhood.

Vandalism

Here are some important facts about vandalism:

- National estimates of damage caused by vandalism are over $1 billion.
- In any given month, one in four schools suffers from vandalism.
- Each incident of school vandalism costs an average of $81.
- Vandals usually work in groups. These groups are predominantly male, but females have become increasingly involved in destructive acts.
- In 1989, 39 percent of the 247,802 arrests for vandalism involved people under 18 years of age.

What Are the Costs and Who Are the Victims of Vandalism?

The idea that vandalism is just mischief and has no real victim is a popular one. The term *victimless crimes* refers to illegal acts that do not specifically harm an individual.

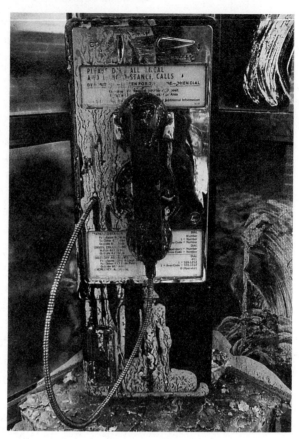

The notion that vandalism is a victimless crime overlooks the fear and outrage felt by those whose property has been intentionally and unjustifiably destroyed, as well as the costs of repairing or replacing vandalized property.

This idea that vandalism doesn't really hurt anyone ignores the anger, fear, and outrage that people feel when their property is deliberately destroyed for no apparent reason. It also ignores the enormous costs involved in repair, cleanup, and replacement of vandalized property.

Vandalism against public structures, such as schools or government buildings, is sometimes prevented by **environmental design**. This term describes actions that control access to a building, help keep watch over it, or manage the way the building is used in order to help prevent vandalism. Environmental design can include anything from placement of outside lighting and landscaping to installation of fences, gates, and security systems. The costs of these actions are sometimes significant, but they are a sound investment in crime prevention.

Private apartment and office buildings also use these techniques. The costs of implementing them are usually passed on to the tenants.

In Your Community

1. Take a look at the way your school or another local public building is designed (the placement of lighting, exits, bushes, fences, and so on). Try to determine how some of those design features might encourage or allow vandalism. Have you noticed problems in your school building lately that are the result of vandalism? If so, make a list of environmental design actions you could recommend to discourage further vandalism.
2. Consider acts that you think fall under the definition of vandalism. How often do you witness the results of someone's intentional destruction of property? How could vandalism be prevented in your community?

Your Turn

1. "Vandalism is a victimless crime because no one is hurt by it." Discuss this statement. Does it accurately reflect the public attitude toward losses from vandalism?
2. The statistics suggest that teenagers are more likely than any other age group to be victims as well as offenders in incidents of property crime. Discuss the factors that you believe cause teenagers to commit property crimes. What do you think would reduce the number of property crimes committed by teenagers in your community?

Taking Action to Stop Vandalism in Your Community

The following advice will help stop vandalism:

- Don't destroy or deface someone else's property or a public place.
- Report acts of vandalism. Quick repairs and cleanups discourage further damage.
- Clean up a park, vacant lot, or school campus. Plant trees, bushes, and flowers.
- Clean graffiti off walls in schools, libraries, and other public facilities. Make it a group project.

- Write articles for the school newspaper on how the juvenile court treats vandalism.
- Get your social studies class, student council, 4-H group, or club to start an anti-vandalism campaign.
- Start a hot line to report vandalism, in cooperation with police and school officials.
- Help your class conduct a survey of the school's levels of pride and morale. Low levels of pride provide fertile grounds for vandalism.
- Work with Neighborhood Watch to start a "Square Mile" or "Block by Block" program in which teens and others take responsibility for the cleanliness of the area and work with residents to maintain it.

Immediately cleaning up graffiti helps the community look better and discourages further vandalism.

In Your Community

What are the programs in your community that help people protect their property from vandalism and prevent burglaries? How do these programs help?

"Invisible" Property Crime

Making a copy of the latest music cassette for a friend? Photocopying three out of five chapters of a library book? Chances are that you are breaking the copyright law. This law protects the right of the person who creates something—anything that is written, sung, painted, photographed, or performed—to use his or her creation and to permit (or refuse to permit) others to use it. "Invisible" property crime refers to property crime that is not obvious or easily seen.

Copyrights protect things that are created. **Patents** offer similar protection to inventions. By giving the inventor or creator the right to determine who can use the material (and to charge a fee for use if desired), our legal system encourages more people to create and invent things of value. Copyrights generally last 50 years and can be renewed; patents last for 17 years.

A New Tool in Property Crime

The personal computer can be both a tool to commit property crime and a target of property crime. One example of this is "phone phreaking," which involves setting up a phone program that tricks the phone system and steals long-distance phone service. Another example is "hacking," which involves using phone lines to dial up a computer system and search for a password in order to gain illegal entry into a system and do some damage.

Some criminals have developed destructive programs such as "viruses" that multiply and clog the system. "Browsers" use hacking to get access to other computers, where they can change or "trash" data. These crimes can be deadly. One hacker who browsed a hospital data base decided to change a patient's medical record. That change caused the patient's death.

Software piracy—making unauthorized copies of copyrighted software programs—is a major threat to our future. The creator of the program gets no pay when copies are stolen; this prospect can discourage people from writing new software. If enough people are discouraged, then exciting new possibilities for computers that could help us all will go unexplored.

How can these crimes be prevented? There are many technical approaches to blocking computer crime, including the use of secure passwords, special electronic devices to scramble signals and decode them, and software that can't be copied. The computer industry has formed active partnerships with law enforcement agencies and prosecuting attorneys to push for swift and certain punishment of those who break the law. But such simple measures as unplugging modems (which are the telecommunications links for computers), storing diskettes securely, and treating computer passwords as absolutely confidential can help a lot.

Looking Back

You and your family live in an apartment building on the East Side. Your family and many of your neighbors, who have lived there a long time, belong to the tenants' organization that has been active in your neighborhood. In the past two years, property crime has increased dramatically in the neighborhood. The people in your building have become increasingly anxious about the safety of their property. You have been selected to sit on the new Property Crime Prevention Task Force of the tenants' organization. Consider the types of property crime and the places where property seems to be most vulnerable. What strategies would you suggest to combat property crime? How would you handle arson and vandalism? Develop a list of recommendations that the task force can present to the owners of the building to help decrease the likelihood of property theft and vandalism.

Role-play a meeting between the task force and the owners of the building where you are presenting your recommendations for preventing property crime. What questions would the tenants want to ask? What questions would the owners want to ask? What action might be taken as a result of the meeting?

5

Criminal and Juvenile Justice

Words to Know

criminal justice
   process
damages
probable cause
evidence
interrogations
search warrant
booking
bail
recognizance
cross-examine
indictment
venue
plea bargaining
rehabilitation
restitution
mandatory
   sentencing
victim impact
   statements
juvenile justice
   system
indeterminate
   sentencing
capital punishment

Objectives

As a result of this chapter you should be able to:

- Define the criminal justice process

- Define the role of the prosecution in the process

- Define the role of the victim in the process

- Discuss the differences between the juvenile and adult systems

- Discuss the nature of sentencing and purposes of punishment

Use Your Experience	List all the people you have seen or met who work as part of the local criminal justice system.

What Is the Criminal Justice Process?

The **criminal justice process** is the system by which violations of laws are reported, suspected offenders are apprehended, and guilt or innocence is established under the law. The process begins when the crime is reported and continues through the arrest, conviction, and confinement of the accused person, ending when he or she is free of control by the state. Because of the value Americans place on freedom, many protections are built into the process to safeguard the person accused of a crime.

In this chapter, the term *criminal justice* generally applies to cases in which adults are accused of a crime. When teens are accused of a crime, they usually go through the juvenile justice system. In some states, courts can decide to treat juveniles above a certain age (often 16) as adults when these youths commit serious crimes.

Criminal Law

A major goal of the law is to regulate human conduct so that people can live together peacefully. As a society, we have designated courts and legislative bodies to establish the laws (rules) that regulate our behavior toward each other. Most laws either forbid (prohibit) certain behavior or require specific action.

In our legal system, most criminal cases are given titles—for example, *The State of Ohio* v. *John Doe*, the accused. The criminal act is considered an act against the state with the victim as witness. The criminal who is found guilty is punished by the state, not by an individual. Under some circumstances, a victim may be able to bring a civil lawsuit against the criminal for **damages** caused by the crime. *Damages* is the legal word used to describe either injuries or losses suffered by one person because of the fault of another. Damages can also refer to the money requested by a court order to compensate for those losses or injuries. However, this may have little meaning if the criminal has no money. Civil lawsuits usually involve a problem between individuals or groups of individuals, rather than between the state and an accused person.

Costs of Criminal Justice

Crime is a major issue in our society not only because of the fear it creates but also because of the costs it brings. According to the U.S. Department of Justice, $61 billion was spent on criminal justice in 1988, an increase of 34 percent over 1985 spending levels. Almost half of the total justice expenditure was for police protection, about 30 percent was spent on the corrections system, and 22 percent was spent on courts and legal services.

Treatment of Victims

In the late 1970s, some victims of crimes began to speak out against inequities between the treatment of the accused and the treatment of the victim in the criminal justice system. Some people thought too much attention was paid to defendants' rights at the expense of victims' rights.

After collecting information and testimony from criminal justice professionals and from victims, the President's Task Force on Victims of Crime made recommendations for the improvement of our criminal justice system. Since 1982, the federal government and many state governments have implemented some of the recommendations. Many of these recommendations will be discussed in this chapter.

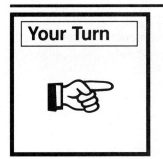

Your Turn

1. Suppose a person is arrested for mugging a teenager. What costs are involved in locating, convicting, and locking up a criminal? Who pays these costs?
2. Consider the costs necessary to reimburse a teenager who has been mugged and robbed. What will it cost to put that person back into the same position he or she was in before the crime? Can all costs be reimbursed? What types of costs are difficult to reimburse?

What Happens When a Crime Is Committed?

Not all crimes result in arrest, and not all arrested people are convicted and sentenced. Throughout the criminal justice process, many suspects are released for a variety of reasons. The prosecutor plays a major role in the progress of a suspect through the system. The prosecutor is the lawyer who represents the government in the case against the defendant.

Following are some of the reasons cases drop out of the system:

- There is insufficient evidence to convict.
- Witnesses refuse to testify.
- Evidence cannot be used because it was illegally obtained by police (for example, through unreasonable search and seizure or forced confessions).
- The case is not brought to trial quickly enough to comply with the U.S. Constitution's Sixth Amendment right to a speedy trial.

The next few pages describe the criminal justice processes for both the accused and the victim.

When a crime is reported, the police are usually the first to respond, so they see the victim when he or she is most in need of help. The President's Task Force on Victims of Crime recommended training programs to ensure that police are:

- Sensitive to the needs of victims
- Informed about existing local services and programs for victims
- Supportive of victims' involvement in these programs and services.

A suspect can be taken into custody with a warrant or without a warrant if the officer has probable cause. **Probable cause** is the officer's reasonable belief that a crime was committed by the suspect.

Your Turn

1. Imagine that you have been robbed at gunpoint. Write a paragraph to complete the following sentence: "After I was robbed, I felt. . ." What could be done to help a person experiencing such feelings?
2. Role-play an interview between a police officer and a teenager who has been robbed. What type of information would be most important for the teenager to hear? What would be most important to the police officer?

In Your Community

1. What number do you call to report a crime in your community?
2. Are police in your community trained to handle the first contact with victims?
3. What programs are available to help victims in your community?

Looking for Evidence

During the investigative stage of the criminal justice process, law enforcement officers have several different methods they can use to obtain information or **evidence** about the crime. These methods include searches, **interrogations**, and confessions.

Citizens are protected from unreasonable search and seizure by the Fourth Amendment of the U.S. Constitution. A **search warrant** is usually required before a search may be made. Law enforcement officers who desire a search warrant must go to a judge and establish probable cause or good reason for the search. However, suspects may be searched at the time of a lawful arrest without a search warrant. Following are some other exceptions to the search warrant requirement:

- Confronting a suspicious person who may be armed (stop and frisk)
- When a person voluntarily consents to a search
- If an object connected to a crime is in plain view
- When police are in hot pursuit of a suspect
- When police have reasonable cause to believe that a vehicle contains contraband (illegal goods)
- In emergency situations
- At borders and in airports.

The U.S. Supreme Court has ruled that evidence obtained by the police in an unreasonable search may not be used at trial. In order to keep illegally obtained evidence out of the trial, the lawyer for the defendant makes a request to the judge at a pretrial hearing. The request, or motion, is based on a legal doctrine commonly referred to as the exclusionary rule (which means the evidence will be excluded, or left out, of the trial).

Interrogations and confessions are an important part of the investigative process. Specific protections are extended to citizens under the Fifth and Sixth Amendments to the U.S. Constitution.

The Fifth Amendment protects citizens against self-incrimination. This means that suspects have the right to remain silent and cannot be forced to testify against themselves.

Under the Sixth Amendment, the suspect has the right to the assistance of an attorney.

Confessions must be voluntary and trustworthy. Police must read the suspect reminders of his or her constitutional rights if they want to use the confession in court.

The courts have held that "Miranda warnings" must be given when a person is questioned, either as a suspect or under arrest.

The name Miranda comes from a Supreme Court case in which the warnings were declared mandatory in certain situations. Ordinarily, the Miranda warnings are given in the following form:

Miranda Warnings

- You have the right to remain silent. Anything you say can be used against you in court.
- You have the right to a lawyer and to have one present while you are being questioned.
- If you cannot afford a lawyer, one will be appointed for you before any questioning begins.

During the investigative process, the victim's property that was involved in the crime may often be taken by the police and held as evidence. Because it is sometimes difficult for the victim to retrieve this property, all property should be carefully marked with the owner's name.

The President's Task Force on Victims of Crime recommended prompt return of the victim's property by the police with the approval of the prosecutor. By 1989, 43 states had laws requiring the prompt return of a victim's property.

Law enforcement personnel need to be trained to understand the needs of victims and to treat them properly. The reaction of victims of violent crime is sometimes treated by police as hysteria. On the other hand, when a nonviolent crime occurs, it is sometimes difficult for police to believe the victim has been truly injured.

Many local law enforcement agencies have now developed specific procedures for dealing with victims of crime. While it may be obvious that sensitivity and tact are important, these may be very difficult to implement.

Your Turn

1. List the important protections for the accused that are part of the initial stages of the criminal justice process. Why are these protections important?
2. What issues do you think are most important to victims during the initial stages of the criminal justice process?
3. Brainstorm a checklist that could be used by police when responding to a victim at the scene of a crime.

In Your Community

Are there any special policies or programs in your community directed at identification of property?

Booking and Initial Appearance, Bail, and Pretrial Release

After arrest, the police "book" the accused. This **booking** consists of making a formal record of the arrest. At this time, the accused is advised of his or her rights, and the charges are explained.

Our system of justice presumes innocence until guilt is admitted or proved at trial.

Bail may be set at this time. Arrested persons may be released after putting up a certain amount of money, called bail, to ensure their presence at trial. The Eighth Amendment to the Constitution protects the accused against the setting of excessive bail. Bail is not always required. Sometimes the court accepts the promise of the accused that he or she will appear at trial. This is called being released on one's own **recognizance**.

Sometimes victims report that they are threatened and intimidated by defendants during this stage. In some states courts order the accused person to stay away from the victim as a condition of pretrial release. If that order is violated, then the accused may be jailed until the trial.

The President's Task Force recommended that police officers give a high priority to investigation of reports of victim/witness intimidation and that they forward these reports to the prosecution. The task force also recommended that prosecutors pursue these charges to the full extent of the law.

Victims should be specially counseled on their role as witnesses before any court appearance. Victim/witness agencies will sometimes help a victim move to a protected location to avoid harassment by the accused.

Preliminary Hearing and Grand Jury

During this stage, the prosecution tries to determine whether there is enough evidence to bring the defendant to trial. At the preliminary hearing, the accused has the right to an attorney and may call and **cross-examine** witnesses. Cross-examination means that the witness is questioned by the opposing side of the case. If a judge dismisses a case at this stage, the prosecutor can still take the case to the grand jury.

In some states a grand jury decides, on the basis of facts presented by the prosecutor, whether there is sufficient cause to believe that a person has committed a crime and should stand trial. If the grand jury believes there is sufficient cause, then it will issue a formal charge. This is called an **indictment**. The Fifth Amendment to the U.S. Constitution requires a grand jury indictment before trial for any serious federal crime. In some states the prosecutor proceeds by filing a formal accusation called a *criminal information*, which details the nature and circumstances of the charge.

The Task Force on Victims of Crime recommended that prosecutors accept the responsibility for informing victims about the status of their cases and that they develop victim and witness on-call systems so as not to waste victims' time.

The Task Force also recommended separate waiting rooms for witnesses for the prosecution and witnesses for the defense. By 1989, 31 states had mandated separate waiting rooms.

Your Turn

1. Why would a crime victim want to keep up with the progress of the case?
2. What information should police and prosecutors explain to victims about the case?

Pretrial Motions and Plea Bargaining

If the accused has been indicted by a grand jury based on sufficient evidence, he or she then makes a court appearance with an opportunity to plead, or respond to the charge. If the accused pleads guilty, the sentencing date is set. If the accused pleads not guilty, the trial date is set.

Once a trial date is set, the accused's lawyer may file pretrial motions. Each motion is a formal request for the court to make a decision or take some action before the trial begins. Pretrial motions can be related to a change in the location of the trial (called a change of **venue**), to evidence, or to additional time for preparation. The court must act on all these motions before the trial can begin.

Many cases never go to trial because of **plea bargaining**. This process involves granting concessions (such as less severe charges) to the accused in exchange for a guilty plea. Plea bargaining avoids the time and costs of a public trial. During this stage, the victim needs to know what alternatives are being discussed by the prosecutor and the defense attorney.

Once the trial begins, victims and witnesses may face several difficult situations. For example, the defendant will be in the courtroom, and it may be painful or upsetting for a victim to see him or her again. Witnesses may have to miss work or school in order to testify. They may also feel frightened or pressured by others not to testify. The prosecutor and police can help if they are informed of these problems. Remember that victims need support and encouragement from family and friends. We have a duty to help make our community a better and safer place to live.

The Task Force on Victims of Crime recommended that prosecutors regularly discuss the case with victims and provide progress reports. This includes taking the victim's views into account before accepting a plea bargain.

By 1989, 31 states had enacted legislation to require that victims be notified of defendants' release on bail, request for a plea bargain, sentencing hearing, and other court procedures.

Your Turn

Are witnesses always enthusiastic about testifying in a criminal case? Why or why not? What can be done to help them feel more comfortable?

Trial and Sentencing

Cases that are not resolved beforehand will go to trial. At trial, several constitutional rights protect the accused. The Sixth Amendment provides for a speedy trial, a right to confront the accuser and cross-examine witnesses, and a right to counsel (an attorney). The Fifth Amendment provides for freedom from self-incrimination.

The prosecutor needs to have enough evidence to convince a jury that the defendant is guilty "beyond a reasonable doubt"—the standard in criminal cases. If the defendant is found guilty, the next phase is sentencing. Judges consider many factors in sentencing, including their own theory of corrections and the best interests of society and the individual.

Over the years, sentencing has served several different purposes. The major purposes of sentencing include:

- Punishment and retribution—The criminal should pay a debt to society for the crime. The sentence serves as official retribution for the wrongful act.
- Incapacitation—The criminal is removed from society. By keeping the criminal locked up, law-abiding citizens are protected.
- Individual deterrence—The sentence should teach the criminal a lesson that discourages him or her from committing another crime.
- General deterrence—The offender should be punished to discourage other people from committing crimes. By punishing criminals, we set a standard for the community.
- **Rehabilitation**—Criminals should be helped to overcome the social, educational, or psychological problems that caused them to commit the crime. Correctional institutions should change the criminal into a law-abiding citizen.

Sentences can include jail (short-term sentences), fines, **restitution**, drug or alcohol abuse treatment programs, and other actions required by the court.

Almost half a million people are in prison (long-term sentences) in the United States today. Many states are sentencing criminals to longer terms. **Mandatory sentencing** laws require terms of a certain length for specified crimes.

Many victims want to stay involved with the case. The President's Task Force on Victims of Crime recommended that victims be notified of the outcomes of proceedings and that judges give appropriate weight to input from victims when sentencing.

By 1989, 48 states had mandated consideration of the effects of the crime on the victim. These effects are formally presented in **victim impact statements**, which can include information about the physical, financial, and emotional injuries caused by the soon-to-be sentenced offender.

Some people are concerned that the use of these statements injects personal revenge into the criminal justice system. Others think these statements introduce too much emotion into the sentencing process. Victim advocates, on the other hand, urge that the impact on victims be one of several factors considered in sentencing.

| **In Your Community** | 1. Prison overcrowding is a national problem. Is it a problem in your state? Discuss some possible solutions to prison overcrowding. |

1. Prison overcrowding is a national problem. Is it a problem in your state? Discuss some possible solutions to prison overcrowding.
2. Evaluate your community's response to victims of crime. What services are available? Are there any gaps in service?
3. Are victim impact statements prepared in your community? Should they be?

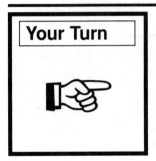

Your Turn

Pervis Payne was convicted by a jury of two counts of first-degree murder and one count of assault with intent to commit first-degree murder.

Payne was convicted of stabbing to death a woman and her two-year-old daughter. A second child was also stabbed and nearly died from the wounds. During the sentencing phase of the trial, the jury heard testimony from four witnesses on behalf of defendant Payne: his mother and father, a good friend, and a clinical psychologist specializing in criminal court evaluation work. The state presented testimony from the maternal grandmother, who told of the murders' devastating effect on the child who survived the attack. The prosecutor stated in his closing remarks that the surviving child "is going to want to know what happened to his baby sister and his mother. He is going to want to know what type of justice was done. . . . With your verdict you will provide the answer."

The jury sentenced Payne to death on each of the murder counts. The defendant sought to appeal the decision, arguing that the grandmother's testimony and the prosecutor's closing argument were unfair and should not have been presented for the jury's consideration.

1. What are the arguments against letting the jury hear the prosecution's closing statements?
2. What are the arguments for letting the jury hear the prosecution's statements?

3. If you were the judge, how would you rule on the defense attorney's appeal, and why?

4. Would your answer be different if the case had concerned an armed robbery for which the penalty was a possible prison term and not the death penalty? Why or why not?

Your Turn

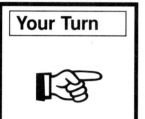

1. Why does society punish criminal offenders? What are the purposes of sentencing?

2. List the purposes of sentencing in order, from most important to least important. Explain your ranking.

Your Turn

Listed below are nine points that the President's Task Force on Victims of Crime recommended. Choose the three points that you believe are the most important and write a paragraph on another sheet of paper in support of your choices. Then choose the three that you consider least important and write a paragraph explaining your reasons.

1. Training programs should be conducted for police and others in the government who deal with victims of crime so that public servants will be more sensitive to victims' needs and more supportive and knowledgeable of services for victims.

2. Recovered property of the victim should be returned promptly by the police with the approval of the prosecution.

3. High priority should be given to police investigations of reports of intimidation of witnesses and to the pursuit of such charges by prosecutors.

4. Victims should be specially counseled on their roles as witnesses prior to any court appearance.

5. Prosecutors should be responsible for informing victims about the status of cases, providing progress reports, and for developing victim and witness on-call systems.

6. There should be separate waiting rooms for the accused and the victims.

7. Criminal justice proceedings should include consideration of the effect of the crime on the victim.
8. Victims should be notified of the outcomes of proceedings.
9. Parole boards should notify victims and their families of parole hearing dates and should allow victim impact statements to be prepared for the board's consideration.

Juvenile Justice

In America, juveniles make up 14 percent of the population. In 1989, 27 percent of all those arrested for serious crimes were under age 18. As youth crime has grown, so has interest in the **juvenile justice system**. Today, most juveniles who commit crimes are treated differently from adults. The goals of juvenile court differ from those of adult court. The juvenile system emphasizes guidance and rehabilitation. However, the epidemic of juvenile crime has caused many people to call for reform of the juvenile justice system.

Juvenile court emphasizes guidance and rehabilitation.

Juvenile courts have not always existed. Until 1899, children who broke the law were treated as adults. However, many people strongly disagreed with the way young people were treated and worked hard to change the law. Special courts were developed to help rather than punish children. In juvenile courts today, young people are considered to be in need of aid, correction, encouragement, and guidance.

State laws vary, but in most places, a juvenile is any person under age 18. Once the juvenile court has jurisdiction over a youth, he or she can remain under the court's supervision until the age of 21 (or 22 or 23 in some states).

Juvenile Court

Juvenile courts handle three types of cases:

1. Delinquency—A juvenile breaks a criminal law. For example, a child is delinquent if he or she steals a car.
2. Status offense—A young person breaks a special law that applies only to juveniles. He or she is generally considered to be in need of special attention. The federal government has developed rules that prohibit states from putting such youths into secure institutions. Status offenders are not considered delinquents.

   Examples of status offenses are:

   - Running away from home
   - Skipping school—The law requires juveniles to attend school until a certain age, often 16.
   - Repeatedly disobeying parents—If parents feel they can no longer control the behavior of their child, the court can remove the child from his or her home.
3. Abuse and neglect—A child is mistreated or ignored by his or her family.

Differences Between Juvenile and Adult Criminal Justice

The juvenile justice system differs from the adult criminal justice system in some terminology* and procedures.

In juvenile court a person:	In adult court a person:
• Is taken into custody or arrested	• Is arrested
• Commits an offense	• Commits a crime

*These terms may differ from state to state.

- Is called a respondent
- Is found delinquent or involved
- Receives a disposition
- Is released from an institution into aftercare.

- Is called a defendant
- Is found guilty
- Receives a sentence
- Is released from prison on parole.

The Case of Gerald Gault

Gerald Gault, age 15, was taken into custody and accused of making an obscene phone call to a neighbor. At the time Gerald was taken into custody, his parents were at work, and the police did not notify them of what had happened to their son. Gerald was placed in a detention center. When his parents finally learned that he was in custody, they were told that there would be a hearing the next day, but they were not told the nature of the complaint against him.

Mrs. Cook, the woman who had complained about the phone call, did not show up at the hearing. Instead, a police officer testified to what he had been told by Mrs. Cook. Gerald blamed the call on a friend and denied making the obscene remarks. No lawyers were present, and no record was made of what was said at the hearing.

Since juries were not allowed in juvenile court, the hearing was held before a judge, who found by a preponderance of the evidence that Gerald was delinquent. The judge ordered him sent to a state reform school until age 21. An adult found guilty of the same crime could be sent to a county jail for no longer than 60 days.

Your Turn

Make a list of anything that happened to Gerald Gault that you consider unfair. Explain your reasoning for each item on the list.

The *Gault* Decision

In deciding the *Gault* case, the U.S. Supreme Court held that juveniles being tried as delinquents and in danger of losing their freedom were entitled to many of the same rights as adult offenders.

Specifically, the Court ruled that juveniles charged with a delinquent act were entitled to be notified of the charges against them, to be represented by an attorney, to confront and cross-examine witnesses, and to remain silent.

When Is a Juvenile Treated as an Adult?

There are times when a juvenile is treated as an adult by the criminal justice system. This means that the juvenile is tried in an adult court and receives an adult punishment. Usually, only older teenagers who are charged with very serious crimes such as armed robbery or murder are treated as adults. Nevertheless, even younger juveniles may be tried in an adult court if they have a long record of serious offenses. Once juveniles are treated as adults by the criminal justice system for a certain crime, they usually will be considered adults for any further crimes they commit.

In Your Community

1. Can juveniles be transferred to adult court in your state? If so, at what age and under what circumstances?
2. How does your state deal with juveniles who repeatedly commit crimes?

Sentencing for Juveniles

Juveniles are usually treated differently from adults in sentencing. In most states, they are given **indeterminate sentences**, meaning they are not given a specific amount of time to serve in an institution. Instead, they will be released when they are found to be rehabilitated. They can stay under the jurisdiction of the court until age 18 or 21, depending on the state. In some states, juveniles must be released after a maximum amount of time (for example, two or three years), or a judge reviews their case periodically (for example, each year).

The federal government, which has been concerned about the mixing of juveniles and adults in county and city jails, encourages the separation of the two groups for the protection of juveniles.

Read the following cases. Assume that the law allows sentences ranging from probation to confinement in an institution from the time of conviction until age 21. Discuss and decide on a sentence for each case.

1. Michael, age 15, was found guilty of burglarizing a home while the owners were at work. He was working with two other men, ages 19 and 21. Detectives who searched a garage rented by the 21-year-old found eight color television sets, seven stereos, four video recorders, and large quantities of jewelry and silverware. Michael has no past record.

2. Walter, age 16, was a member of a four-person team that robbed a convenience store. During the holdup, one of the employees panicked and was shot by one of the other robbers. Walter had dropped out of high school.

3. Leisha, age 15, was found guilty of possession of three grams of cocaine. The drugs were spotted by a security guard while she was at her locker. Leisha has no prior record.

4. Jerry, age 17, was found guilty of selling drugs at an elementary school playground. Jerry has dropped out of high school.

Capital Punishment

Capital punishment (the death penalty) is the most severe and controversial sentence in the United States today. As of 1991, more than 36 states have laws that authorize the use of the death penalty in certain cases. The laws require the judge and jury to consider any factors that might affect the seriousness of the offense. These are known as aggravating or mitigating factors.

Opponents of capital punishment argue that it is morally wrong to take the life of anyone, even someone convicted of murder. They contend that the death penalty does not deter crime. In support of this contention, they cite studies showing that most murders result from fear, passion, mental disorder, or anger of the moment. They say the death penalty is no more a deterrent than the possibility of a long prison term. Opponents also point to the possibility of executing an innocent person.

Those favoring the use of capital punishment point to opinion polls indicating that most Americans favor the death penalty and say it is morally justifiable to take the life of a convicted murderer.

They also argue that it does deter crime and that it saves the government the cost of keeping convicted murderers in prison for long periods of time.

Capital Punishment for Juveniles

One of the most difficult questions involving the death penalty is whether it should be imposed on juveniles who commit murder.

Our juvenile justice system focuses on the rehabilitation of youth. In most other countries, people who kill while under the age of 18 are spared the death penalty. But in the United States, as a result of a case handed down by the Supreme Court in 1988, if an individual state has set a minimum age limit for execution, then that state can use the death penalty as a sentence. The Court affirmed that juveniles who are 16 years old and who commit capital murder can be subjected to the death penalty. The decision about the use of capital punishment for juveniles is left up to state law and varies from state to state. As of 1991, 26 states permitted the execution of juveniles under the age of 17.

In Your Community

1. Does your state allow the death penalty? Do you favor or oppose the death penalty for adult crimes? For juvenile crimes?
2. Design a survey and poll your schoolmates on this issue.

Looking Back

Assume that you are a judge and you must decide whether a juvenile who committed an armed robbery should be tried as a juvenile or as an adult. What questions would you ask about the juvenile in order to help you make your decision?

6

Conflict Management

Words to Know

conflict
assault
personal conflict
   management
negotiation
mediation
mediator
disputant
resolution/resolve
agreement
   (contract)
triggers
active listening
options
brainstorm

Objectives

As a result of this chapter you should be able to:

- Define conflict

- Describe conflict management and mediation

- Identify your triggers

- Use active listening skills

- Generate options in the face of conflict

- Understand the potential use of conflict management skills in your school and community

Use Your Experience

Do you know people who cannot control their temper or who let conflict build up inside until they are almost ready to explode? What effect does this behavior have on them and on the people around them? Does it affect their ability to perform at school or work? How does it affect their relationships with friends, family, coworkers, or classmates?

What Is Conflict?

Many violent crimes result from conflicts between people who know one another. The word **conflict** comes from the Latin word *conflictus*, meaning "striking together." When we say we are in conflict with another person, we usually mean we have had some type of hostile encounter. (Confrontation with an armed criminal is not a type of conflict you should seek to manage according to the material presented in this chapter.)

Conflicts can range from an argument with your sister or brother to an **assault** (an intentional threat or attempt to inflict bodily injury). Conflict is a part of everyday life. We bump into people on the bus, drop a book on someone's foot in math class, spill catsup on the lunch table and fail to clean it up before a friend puts her elbow in it. Sometimes it seems like we are constantly involved in some type of conflict. The question is not whether there is going to be conflict in your life, but how to handle it when it comes up.

Arguments are a type of conflict. Conflict is sometimes difficult to deal with because of the relationship issues and intense emotions that come up. In many cases arguments lead to assault. One simple way to protect yourself is to refuse to allow the other party to pressure you into losing control. When we think of assault, we often picture a surprise attack by a stranger. However, most assaults involve people who know each other.

Your Turn

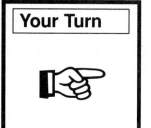

Li and Bob, who know each other slightly, were assigned to share a locker. During the last few weeks, Bob has become increasingly irritated because Li leaves the locker messy and because she borrows his books without asking permission. Bob has tried to ignore the problem because Li has been helping him complete some science homework. Today, however, Bob went to the locker and found that his math book was missing again. He found Li in the hallway and started yelling at her. One thing led to another, and soon there was shoving and fighting.

1. How would you define the problem between Li and Bob?
2. Look at the line that follows. Already listed on the line are two ways to resolve the problem. Think of two additional ways in which Bob and Li could resolve their problem without involving the principal or any school adult. Plot your additional solutions on the line where you think they belong.

fight   flight
_____

3. Form pairs and choose a part in the role-play (Bob or Li). Each pair has three minutes to discuss the dispute and come up with a resolution. If no resolution is reached, Bob and Li will have to go to the principal's office. After you have discussed possible resolutions with your partner, use these questions to consider the issues with the rest of the class:

   • How many of you were able to resolve the dispute?
   • What were some of the solutions?
   • How many of you will be going to see the principal?
   • Do any of the suggested solutions require the help of an outside person?
   • What are the pros and cons of each possible solution?

Who Has the Energy to Resolve a Dispute?

Every day each of us faces conflicts that need resolving. All individuals use dispute resolution processes during the course of a day. Dispute resolution can range from an informal "I'm sorry . . ." to a formal trip to police headquarters. Sometimes we are able to resolve conflicts ourselves and sometimes we need help. **Personal conflict management** consists of two (or more) people working together to resolve their problem. This process of discussing an issue in order to reach an agreement is also called **negotiation**. Both people must want to settle their disagreement before it becomes a larger one. Learning the skills necessary to manage conflict can help people cooperate in order to handle problems better. These skills are discussed later in this chapter.

Mediation is another form of conflict management. It involves a neutral third person, called a **mediator**, who assists the **disputants** in resolving their problem. Only the disputants themselves, not the mediator, can actually resolve the problem. Mediations are usually confidential. One of the mediator's most important tasks is to help separate the real interests of the disputants from their stated positions. What a person states as wants or needs might be different than the person's real interests. For example, a disputant might state the position, "We must eat at six o'clock" when the person's real interest is to attend a basketball game at 7:30. The mediator encourages the disputants to discuss issues beyond their stated positions in order to try to get a complete picture of the conflict. It is easy to get sidetracked, allowing the positions of the disputants to get in the way of developing a resolution. If the disputants are not encouraged to discuss their real interests, the resolution will be built on shaky ground.

With the help of the mediator, parties voluntarily communicate their feelings and positions. Once the dispute is clear, the parties can discuss solutions to the conflict. This **resolution,** or **agreement**, which usually takes the form of a **contract**, is signed by both parties. The mediation process emphasizes resolving the conflict, not placing the blame for it. The resolution should focus on the future relationship between the two parties. The actual steps in the process are explained at the end of this chapter.

In the locker-sharing dispute between Bob and Li, the principal's involvement is a form of dispute resolution with which students are familiar. Once the principal is involved, the energy and power to resolve the problem shift, and the principal becomes responsible for settling the dispute.

In both personal conflict management and mediation, the ideas for resolving the problem come mainly from the disputants themselves. In both these processes, the energy to resolve the dispute comes from the people who have the problem and not from an outside source. This way they take responsibility for their actions and work out the problem without physical contact. Such solutions are also more likely to work than those that come from the outside.

Your Turn

1. Why do you think that conflict management often works better when the solution comes from the people having the conflict?
2. Can you think of any other examples of disputes in which a third party could help to resolve the problem? Make a list of some examples.
3. Analyze the list you have made to see who should resolve the conflict in each case. Should it be the people with the problem, or the person who intervenes?

What Role Do Courts Play in Conflict Management?

Courts play an important role in resolving conflicts in our society, but there are many other ways to settle disputes. In reality, only a small number of disputes ever get to court. In the past few years, other forms of dispute resolution have become increasingly popular.

Two reasons for this trend are that the many cases coming to court create a backlog, and often a judge is unable to propose a creative resolution that will meet the needs of the parties. Frequently the relationship between the plaintiff and the defendant is strained or severed during the course of a court case. Some disputants feel that they lose in court even when they win because, win or lose, they must invest a lot of time and money in the court process.

In Your Community

Are there any individuals, organizations, or programs in your community from which people can get help in resolving disputes? If so, develop a list of them. Be sure to include what types of disputes are handled and how a person can make use of the services provided.

Your Turn

The Musaks and the Colemans are neighbors on a quiet street in Newville. They have never gotten along. This is partly because the Musaks' teenage children, Marvin and Maria, have been careless and noisy when entering and leaving their home, and they frequently cut across the Colemans' yard. The Colemans have complained and the Musaks have promised to speak to the children, but the problem has continued. The Musaks are tired of the problem and would like to get along with their neighbors.

Three weeks ago, one of the Musak children destroyed some bushes in front of the Coleman house while trying to park the family car. The Colemans spoke to the Musaks about it and asked for $400 to cover the cost of replacing the bushes. The Musaks said that they would not pay $400. The Musaks feel that the Colemans tend to exaggerate every problem. Last week the Colemans called the police because the Musak children's stereo was turned up. The Colemans' constant complaining is very annoying to the Musak family but the Colemans feel that their complaints are justified. The Coleman family has lived in the neighborhood for many years and would like to resolve the problem.

1. Role-play the situation in which the Coleman family takes the Musaks to court to get them to replace the bushes. One person should play a member of the Coleman family, another a member of the Musak family, and a third the judge. The judge should listen to both sides of the case and then make a decision. After the judge makes the decision, take a moment to write down how you feel about it. Then write down how you think the Musaks and the Colemans feel.

2. Role-play the same situation, except that this time the Colemans and the Musaks try to resolve the problem without involving a judge. The two students who role-play the family members should try to work out a solution to the problem. The third student should watch the role-play carefully and take notes about how well the disputants work together to resolve the problem. After the problem is resolved, take a moment to write down your feelings about the process.

3. Discuss the following questions:

   - What was the decision in the first role-play?
   - How did the Colemans and the Musaks feel about the decision made by the judge? How did you feel about it?
   - What was the outcome when the families tried to resolve the problem by themselves?
   - Which resolution will hold up best? Why?
   - Are there some disputes that would be better handled by a judge in a court process? List some disputes that you feel should be handled by a court.
   - Are there some disputes that two people could handle better by themselves? List some disputes that you feel should be handled in mediation.

4. List the differences between taking a case to court and settling the problem by yourself.

5. Brainstorm a list of skills that might help a disputant manage a conflict.

What Skills Are Involved in Personal Conflict Management?

All types of conflict management involve three important skills:

- Awareness of "triggers"
- Active listening
- Ability to generate options for resolving the conflict.

The next few sections explain these skills and show you how they work.

Triggers

In order to manage conflict successfully, people must understand their own feelings about conflict.

Triggers are any verbal or nonverbal behaviors that result in anger or other emotional reactions. Triggers are like lightning bolts. When they strike, they interfere with the communication between people. Triggers cause disputants to focus on the annoying behavior instead of on the problem they are trying to solve. An awareness of triggers means that we know what types of behavior cause anger in ourselves and others.

Everyone has triggers. For example, some people do not like to have an index finger waved in their face by someone who is

A trigger is a verbal or nonverbal behavior that provokes an emotional reaction, like anger. Such anger can lead to a conflict or can make a conflict harder to resolve.

criticizing them. The wagging finger triggers the person's anger, and then he or she cannot concentrate on the underlying problem. Triggering someone's anger usually makes a problem more difficult to solve.

In order to be able to resolve conflicts in our own lives, we need to understand and recognize the things that make other people angry. Once we are conscious of our own triggers, we can understand when another person exhibits a type of behavior that makes us angry. We can also assume that many of the things that make us angry will have the same effect on other people. To avoid pulling others' triggers, we have to pay particular attention to our own behavior.

Once we see and understand our own triggers, we can take control of our responses. Once we grasp the underlying causes of anger, we can develop the patience and skill to be effective conflict managers. Often, it is helpful to see the problem from another person's perspective. Standing in the shoes of another person can help us discover new ideas for resolution.

Your Turn

1. Write down your answers to the following questions:
   - What are trigger words for me?
   - What kind of body language is a trigger for me?
   - How do I know when I'm angry?
   - How do I react to my triggers?
   - Do I have a long fuse or a short fuse? (Am I slow or quick to anger?)

2. Get together with four other students and discuss your answers. Develop a combined list of the group's triggers.

3. Discuss your group's list of triggers with the rest of the groups in the class. What do you notice about these lists? Are any of the triggers the same? Are any of the other responses to anger the same?

4. What are the advantages and disadvantages of short and long fuses? Is there any advantage to increasing the time it takes you to respond to your triggers? Do you think people have shorter fuses with their families and longer fuses with their friends? Why or why not?

Active Listening

The second skill that is important to conflict management is **active listening**. Good communication requires good listening. The term *active listening* implies that listening requires more than just sitting still and not talking. It requires both hearing and understanding, and showing that you've heard and understood. In conversations we sometimes do not listen closely to what the other person is saying. Instead we jump ahead and think about what we will say when it's our turn to talk. People who are active listeners are able to give other people the feeling that they are really being heard.

Hearing + Understanding = Active Listening

A good listener shows that he or she really hears and understands the speaker.

Good listening requires concentration. Often people can tell if we are listening by the nonverbal cues we give, such as eye contact or a tilt of the head. When a listener is physically attentive, the speaker is more comfortable and able to communicate better. When a speaker is finished, it's a good idea to summarize the message and repeat it back. This feedback should acknowledge the feelings the speaker communicated as well as the verbal message.

In our noisy, fast-paced society, good listening competes with a lot of other activity. In addition, people are sometimes concerned that attentive listening may give the impression that they agree with what the speaker is saying. Even if you disagree with another person, you need to learn how that person views the problem by listening carefully. A speaker may not react as negatively to someone who disagrees if that person has listened carefully. Listening does not mean that you agree with the speaker; it only means that you are paying attention.

We all know how good it feels to have someone listen to our problems, so we need to consider how important it is to respond as a good listener when others come to us. There are lots of verbal and nonverbal ways to give people the idea that you are listening. Asking questions, making eye contact, leaning toward the speaker, summarizing the speaker's thoughts and feelings, having a relaxed manner, and paraphrasing what the person is telling you are just a few. Listening effectively is important to understanding the facts surrounding a conflict.

1. Why don't people listen? List some things that get in the way of careful listening.
2. Develop a list of nonverbal cues that you can give another person to let him or her know that you are listening.
3. What verbal skills can you use that would let a speaker know that you are listening and understanding him or her?
4. Role-play a situation in which two friends are talking. One friend is telling the other about something very important that is going on in her or his life. The other friend is not a good listener and is doing all kinds of things that show that she or he is not listening.

   a. How does the friend who is trying to talk feel about the communication?
   b. What can be done to improve the situation?

Generating Options

The third core skill that is important to conflict management is the ability to generate **options** for resolving a conflict. We all know people who, when faced with a conflict, can only think of two options: fighting or running away. Maybe some of us have even been that person when faced with a conflict in our own lives. The nice thing about analyzing a conflict when you are not involved is that you can think of lots of possibilities because you have plenty of time. When things happen quickly, it is sometimes difficult to think of a broad range of responses.

There are two steps to take when generating options. Once you have all the facts straight, **brainstorm** all the ideas you can that might help solve the problem. At this stage list ideas without deciding if they are good or not. Because you want the best solution, you want the list of options to be as long as possible. At this point there are no dumb ideas or good ideas; there is just a list of ideas. Listing ideas that may not work might even help you think of some that will.

The second step is to discuss each of the ideas and select the ones from the list that best meet the interests of the people involved. Both people should have the opportunity to discuss and evaluate each potential solution. Both should think about the consequences of each solution. This gives them the chance to reflect on the outcome and visualize how the idea will "play out" in real life.

Once the parties agree to a solution with which they both feel comfortable, the conflict will be resolved.

Your Turn

The Noisy Neighbor

Cora lives in a duplex on a quiet street in Shortville. She has enjoyed living there for several years. The house is on the bus line and close to a grocery store. Several months ago, George, a father with two teenagers, Louis and Ana, moved into the upstairs apartment. Now there is a lot more noise in Cora's building. Some evenings the noise makes it impossible for Cora to get to sleep. Cora wants to get along with her new neighbors, but several times she has had to talk to George about the noise. George considers Cora to be a complainer. He knows that the kids should be quieter, but he does not like to keep after them about it.

Last night one of the teens, Louis, came home with a friend from a party around 3:00 A.M. There was a lot of noise in the hallway. Cora was so frustrated that she opened the door and started yelling at the kids. Her yelling triggered Louis' anger and without thinking, he picked up a broom that was in a corner of the hallway and shook it at her. The broom hit one of the little windows in Cora's door and shattered it. Cora called Louis a juvenile delinquent and vowed to call the police.

1. What is the conflict between Cora and her neighbors about?
2. How does Cora feel? How does Louis feel? How does George feel?
3. What is going to happen next if Cora calls the police?
4. Brainstorm four possible solutions for Louis, his father, and Cora.
5. What are the pros and cons of each potential solution? What are the consequences of each suggested action?
6. Does the solution require the involvement of an outside person?
7. Choose the two solutions that are most likely to resolve the problem and keep it from happening again.
8. How would the solution change if Cora were your grandmother?

Steps in Personal Conflict Management

In order to use conflict management skills to help resolve a dispute, you must:

1. Come to the discussion with a sincere interest in settling the problem.
2. Listen carefully to the interests of the other side. Do not let triggers get in the way of listening and understanding. Make sure you know the real concerns of the other person.
3. Use active listening skills. This means that you must hear what is being said and understand it. Good listeners make eye contact, relax, think carefully about what the other person is saying, and ask good questions.
4. Try to think about the problem from the other person's perspective.
5. Think about the issue that is causing the problem, not about the personalities of the people involved. What is the underlying problem? Sort out the facts of the situation from the emotions being raised by each party.

6. Think of as many potential solutions to the problem as possible. Make a list and try not to decide right away whether they are good solutions.
7. Identify solutions that both parties can live with. Concentrate on the reality of the situation.
8. Repeat the main points of the agreement to be sure that both of you understand it. Sometimes it is a good idea to write down the agreement.
9. Agree in advance to discuss the problem again if the agreement does not seem to be working.

Even if you are the only person who understands the concepts involved in conflict management, you can still help resolve a conflict by discussing each part of the process with the other person as you go along.

Your Turn

Role-play a conflict management session between Cora, Louis, and George from the "Noisy Neighbor" scenario. Use the steps listed in this section to help organize the role-play. Students who are not involved in the role-play should be watching to see if the participants make good use of their conflict management skills.

After the role-play, discuss the following questions:

- How did the disputants feel about the process?
- Were the disputants comfortable with the skills involved?
- How did the disputants feel about the outcome?
- Did the observers feel that the disputants were comfortable with the process? What problems and successes did the observers note?
- Will the agreement work?

Mediation

The skills involved in mediation are part of the conflict management process. The mediator helps the people work through the process. A typical mediation is confidential and has the following ground rules:

1. Respect each other.
2. Do not interrupt each other.
3. Agree to work together on resolving this issue.
4. Tell the truth.

The outline that follows describes the steps involved in a mediation session.

Step 1. Introduction

The mediator makes the parties feel at ease and explains the ground rules. The mediator's role is not to make a decision but to help the parties reach agreement. The mediator explains that he or she will not take sides.

Step 2. Telling the Story

Each party tells what happened. The person bringing the complaint tells his or her side of the story first. No interruptions are allowed. Then the other party explains his or her version of the facts. Any of the participants, including the mediators, may take notes during the process. The notes taken by the mediators will be destroyed at the end of the mediation in order to ensure confidentiality.

Step 3. Identifying Facts and Issues

The mediator attempts to identify agreed-upon facts and issues. This is done by listening to each side, summarizing each party's views, and checking to see if each party understands them.

Step 4. Identifying Alternative Solutions

Everyone thinks of possible solutions to the problem. The mediator makes a list and asks each party to explain his or her feelings about each possible solution.

Step 5. Revising and Discussing Solutions

Based on the expressed feelings of the parties, the mediator revises possible solutions and attempts to identify a solution that both parties can agree to.

Step 6. Reaching an Agreement

The mediator helps the parties to reach an agreement that both can live with by choosing a solution that has been discussed and agreed to by both parties. The agreement should be written down. The parties should also discuss what will happen if either of them breaks the agreement.

Looking Back

Use the mediation outline to role-play the two conflict situations that follow. In each conflict situation, two students should play the parts of the people in conflict. Two students should mediate the dispute and help develop an agreement.

Conflict #1

Robert: For four months, 17-year-old Robert has been working as a cashier for a dry cleaner. He sometimes has trouble talking to customers, because he is preoccupied by things on his mind. Robert's boss, Mrs. King, has just overheard a heated exchange between him and a customer. When Robert could not find the customer's shirts, the customer made some rude remarks to him. Robert responded by being rude himself, since he feels that rude people deserve rude treatment. Besides, he did not sleep very well last night. Robert needs and wants to keep his job.

Mrs. King: Mrs. King has spent considerable time training Robert for his job as cashier. Although she likes Robert and is basically pleased with his performance, she also recognizes that he has difficulty talking to customers. Mrs. King has been coaching Robert in making conversation, and his skills have improved over the last four months. Robert's angry exchange with the customer upsets Mrs. King, especially because she has been helping him in this area. She plans to speak with Robert this morning.

Conflict #2

Tom: Tom, a quiet and studious 16-year-old, has liked Latisha for quite a while. Latisha is dating Joe, although she never mentions him to Tom when they walk to class together. Tom is gathering the courage to invite Latisha to a movie. Although he has occasionally fought to defend his younger brother, Tom generally avoids physical confrontation.

Joe: Joe, known around campus as a "tough guy," has been dating Latisha for about three months. Joe considers Latisha "his girl," although he has never told her he thinks of her this way. Joe has been suspended from school several times for fighting. Joe has heard recently that Tom often walks Latisha to class. When Joe called Latisha tonight to invite her to Saturday's drag races, he told her he disliked Tom. He said he hoped Tom would ask her out, just so he could challenge him to a fight. Joe plans to look for Tom at school today.

7

Child Abuse

Words to Know

child abuse
neglect
physical abuse
sexual abuse
pornography
incest
coercion
deceit
emotional abuse
child protective
  service agencies
disclosure

Objectives

As a result of this chapter you should be able to:

■ Define child abuse and neglect

■ Discuss the causes and effects of child abuse and neglect

■ Identify some effective responses to child abuse and neglect

| Use Your Experience | Have you heard a recent news story about child abuse? Why do you think child abuse is sometimes not discovered or reported? |

What Is Child Abuse?

Child abuse includes the physical, sexual, emotional, and verbal abuse or **neglect** of an infant, child, or adolescent. Every state has laws against child abuse. The laws make child abuse a criminal act.

Child abuse and neglect cases are frequently not reported. Many people are reluctant to interfere in the family affairs of others. To help solve this problem, most states require doctors, nurses, teachers, social workers, and, in some cases, the general public to report suspected child abuse cases.

Physical Abuse

Individuals, courts, child protective agencies, and law enforcement agencies often differ over the exact definition of **physical abuse**. All would agree that acts that threaten a child's life or cause serious injury constitute abuse. But many would differ over the line between a spanking, which some consider an acceptable form of discipline, and a beating that escalates into brutality, which is against the law.

Sexual Abuse

Child **sexual abuse** involves an adult or older child using a child for his or her sexual gratification. It can refer to a forced sexual assault on a child victim. It can also refer to sexual contact between a child and another person in which threats, bribery, or other methods involving force are used to get the child to participate. About 90 percent of child victims are abused by someone they know rather than by a stranger. Teens can be both victims and abusers.

Child sexual abuse includes not only offenses in which there is direct physical contact between the offender and the child but also "nontouching" offenses in which the child is persuaded to view obscene materials or is involved in child **pornography**. Pornography includes pictures and writings intended to arouse sexual desire.

What Is Incest?

In most states, **incest** is defined as sexual intercourse between people who are closely related to each other. Incest is more difficult to talk about than sexual assault by a stranger. But it happens to at least 100,000 children and teens each year. The most common kind of incest is sex between an older family member—a parent, stepparent, uncle, or cousin—and a child or teenager. Most victims are girls, although it happens to boys as well.

Incest relies on secrecy. Thus, the best way to stop it is to tell someone. If that person doesn't believe it, then it's necessary to tell someone else and keep telling until someone listens and takes action.

Victims frequently blame themselves for the family crisis brought on by abuse, but it is not their fault. This is a traumatic time for the victim and a time when outside support is essential.

Your Turn

Discuss reasons why incest victims might feel even more shame, anger, and guilt than other victims of sexual assault. Does the victim's dependence on the abuser contribute to this feeling? What does the victim learn about love and loyalty from this experience?

Characteristics of Sexual Assault and Incest

The chief characteristics of incest and many cases of sexual assault include the following:

1. **Coercion**—The child is bribed with treats or threatened with punishment (sometimes harm to a loved one) if she or he fails to comply with the abuser's demands.
2. **Deceit**—The child is often told that the sexual touching is being done because the older person loves the child. This is a lie.
3. **Length of time**—The abuse usually occurs for months or years before the child discloses the events. Four to seven years is not uncommon.
4. **Progression**—The sexual acts increase in seriousness, generally from fondling to intercourse.
5. **Secrecy**—The child has not told anyone what has been happening. It is a closely guarded secret. The adult often warns the child not to tell.

Emotional Abuse

Emotional abuse is less likely to be reported than other forms of abuse. **Emotional abuse** can include swearing, yelling, or insulting a child, often repeatedly. It can also include denying a child's basic emotional needs, such as affection and security. Emotional abuse often accompanies physical and sexual abuse and is considered by experts to be very serious.

Neglect

Failure to provide adequate food, shelter, and supervision for younger children can constitute criminal neglect. This situation can result in removal of the neglected child from the home to the custody of the state.

All forms of child abuse, including emotional abuse, cause the victim real pain and suffering.

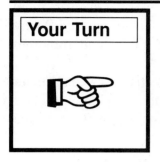

Your Turn

1. Many people feel that information about their family life is private. Society is interested in protecting family privacy, but that must be limited when child abuse occurs. Why does society have a special interest in the protection of children in a family?

2. List responsibilities that parents have to their children. Should there be laws that outline all these responsibilities?

3. How do you think the courts should deal with incest? Are there ways to handle this problem other than through the courts? What is likely to work best for everyone involved?

How Does the Public Feel About Child Abuse?

According to the National Committee for the Prevention of Child Abuse (NCPCA) 1991 annual survey of the attitudes of adults toward child abuse prevention, 75 percent believed that physical punishments can lead to injury to the child. This was a 4 percent increase over 1987. The same survey revealed that 75 percent of the adults also believed that repeated yelling and swearing can lead to long-term emotional problems for a child. As the public begins to understand the problem and its causes, improvements can occur.

Other information provided by the survey included the following:

- From 1987 to 1991, the number of parents who admitted to repeatedly yelling and swearing at their children as a form of discipline declined by 11 percent.
- During the same time period, there was a 12 percent decrease in the number of parents who reported using spanking as a form of discipline. The majority did not, however, consider spanking a form of child abuse.
- Violence between parents and children is not limited to low-income groups, as is commonly believed.

How Widespread Is Child Abuse?

There has been a major increase in reports of child abuse from 1980 to 1990. An estimated 2.5 million children were reported victims of child abuse in 1990. The number of reported child or teen deaths from abuse increased by 38 percent from 1985 to 1990. It is estimated that three children under 18 years of age die from abuse or neglect every day in the United States.

The number of cases is overwhelming, whether there are more actual incidents now or just more cases being reported. Many authorities believe that child abuse is the most underreported crime in the United States.

The 1990 annual survey of **child protective service agencies** (government departments that investigate complaints of child abuse and stop it where they know it exists) in the 50 states and the District of Columbia found:

- Of the 45 states reporting, there was an average 4 percent increase over the previous year in the number of child abuse cases reported.
- Twenty-seven percent of child abuse cases involved physical abuse, 15 percent sexual abuse, 46 percent neglect, 9 percent emotional mistreatment, and 4 percent some other form of abuse.
- Abusers were related to the victim in 95 percent of the cases in the 26 states reporting this information.

Figure 1–Child abuse and neglect reports, 1985-1990

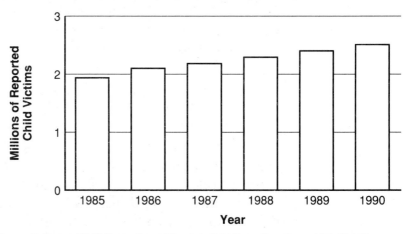

Source: D. Daro and K. McCurdy, *Current Trends in Child Abuse Reporting and Fatalities: The Results of the 1990 Annual 50-State Survey,* 1991.

In Your Community

1. Find out what the child abuse statistics are for your city or county. Has there been an increase since 1985? If so, what is the percent of increase? How does this compare to the national statistics in this chapter?
2. Find out what statutes or guidelines your community's child protective service agency follows when deciding to charge a parent with abuse. What is the policy on emotional abuse and neglect?

3. What programs exist in your area to help abuse victims? Does your community provide shelters where victims can live to avoid abuse at home?

Your Turn	Decide whether you think each of the following statements is true or false:

a. Children make up stories about being sexually molested.
b. Parents should punish their children any way they choose.
c. Children under age 10 (including infants) are rarely sexually assaulted.
d. Usually, the sexual offender is someone unknown to the family.
e. Young children can forget about sexual abuse and are better off if they don't talk about it.
f. Child abusers are likely to stop their abuse even without help.
g. Child abuse is less frequent in higher-income families.

What Are the Causes of Child Abuse?

Authorities believe that while there is no single cause of child abuse, certain characteristics of individuals and problems in society are contributing factors. Authorities generally agree that individuals who were abused as children, those who abuse alcohol or other drugs, those under financial stress, those who have job or unemployment stress, and those lacking skills to deal with conflict without resorting to violence are more likely than other adults to abuse a child.

In the 1990 survey of child protective services agencies, 55 percent of the states that showed increases in the number of child abuse reports mentioned substance abuse as one of the primary causes. Several states said that alcohol abuse represented more of a problem for families under their jurisdiction than abuse of illegal drugs. Thirty-five percent mentioned financial problems, unemployment, and poverty as reasons for higher numbers of reported cases. Other states believed that their efforts to educate the public and to encourage better reporting had increased the number of cases on file.

Adults in the general public tended to emphasize violence between husbands and wives and violent images in the media when asked about the causes of child abuse.

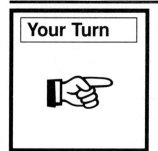

Your Turn

What are the different types of child abuse? What do you think causes child abuse and neglect? Do you think the causes vary for different types of abuse? Why?

Signs of Child Abuse

Child abuse has a serious effect on everyone in the community because of the injustice it does to helpless members of society and the long-term pain it produces. To deal with the problem, we must be able to recognize and report it. Also, as already mentioned, laws in most states require certain people (for example, doctors and teachers) to report suspected child abuse.

None of the signs of child abuse listed here proves that a child is being abused. Many of them may be found in almost any parent or child at one time or another. But when these signs appear repeatedly or in combination, they should cause friends and teachers to take a closer look at the situation and to consider the possibility of child abuse. The second look may reveal further signs of abuse or signs of a particular kind of child abuse.

Some warning signs in children include:

- Sudden changes in behavior or school performance
- No help received for physical or medical problems even when they are brought to the parents' attention
- Watchfulness and wariness as though preparing for something bad to happen
- Behavior that is "too good"—overly compliant, overachieving, or too responsible
- Coming to school early, staying late, and showing a reluctance to go home.

Warning signs in parents include:

- Showing little concern for the child
- Denying the existence of—or blaming the child for—all the child's problems in school, at play, or at home
- Seeing the child as bad, worthless, and burdensome
- Demanding perfection or a level of physical or academic performance the child cannot achieve.

Signs of Physical Abuse

A child who is suffering from physical abuse:

- Has unexplained burns, bites, bruises, broken bones, black eyes, or other marks
- Seems frightened of the parents and protests or cries when it is time to go home from school
- Tells of injury by a parent or another adult caregiver.

Signs of Sexual Abuse

A child who is a victim of sexual abuse:

- Has difficulty walking or sitting
- Describes symptoms suggesting venereal disease
- Demonstrates bizarre, sophisticated, or unusual sexual knowledge or behavior for his or her age
- Reports nightmares, insomnia, or other sleep disturbances.

Signs of Emotional Mistreatment

A child who is suffering emotional abuse:

- May demonstrate extreme behavior, becoming overly passive, compliant, demanding, or aggressive
- May practice either inappropriately adult behaviors, such as parenting other children, or inappropriately infantile behavior, such as frequent rocking or headbanging
- Is much less emotionally developed than other children of the same age.

Signs of General Neglect

A child who is generally neglected:

- May be absent from school frequently
- Begs or steals food or money from classmates
- Is consistently dirty and has severe body odor
- Lacks proper clothing for the weather
- States that there is no one at home to provide care.

Preventing Child Abuse

In recent years, more public attention has been focused on the issue of child abuse, and many organizations and government agencies have increased their efforts to educate the public on the effects of physical, sexual, and emotional abuse of children.

These efforts have done much to prevent additional incidents of abuse. The changes in public attitudes show that education and awareness efforts have been successful.

According to a 1990 public opinion survey, one of every four individuals and one of every three parents took some sort of action to prevent child abuse in 1990. The actions they took included stopping another parent from lashing out at a child, offering assistance to a parent under stress, and contributing to an organization that works to prevent child abuse.

12 alternatives to lashing out at your child.

The next time everyday pressures build up to the point where you feel like lashing out—STOP! And try any of these simple alternatives.

You'll feel better . . . and so will your child.

1. Take a deep breath. And another. Then remember <u>you</u> are the adult . . .

2. Close your eyes and imagine you're hearing what your child is about to hear.

3. Press your lips together and count to 10. Or better yet, to 20.

4. Put your child in a time-out chair. (Remember the rule: one time-out minute for each year of age.)

5. Put yourself in a time-out chair. Think about why you are angry: Is it your child, or is your child simply a convenient target for your anger?

6. Phone a friend.

7. If someone can watch the children, go outside and take a walk.

8. Take a hot bath or splash cold water on your face.

9. Hug a pillow.

10. Turn on some music. Maybe even sing along.

11. Pick up a pencil and write down as many helpful words as you can think of. Save the list.

12. Write for parenting information: Parenting, Box 2866, Chicago, IL 60690.

 Take Time Out. Don't Take It Out On Your Child.

® National Committee for Prevention of Child Abuse

Several states have taken creative and successful actions to prevent child abuse. Hawaii is one of the few states to report steady declines in the numbers of reported cases since 1985. State officials give credit for the decrease to their prevention and intervention programs. In 1985 the state's health department began to assess all newborn babies to determine if there is a significant chance the baby will be abused. Home services to assist families in dealing with stress, follow-ups, and preventive health care for the child until kindergarten are provided to families thought to be at risk. Hawaii is the only state to offer such comprehensive services to a majority of its families.

In other states, prevention programs often focus on substance abuse. Examples of several 1991 programs include:

- California—The California Trust Fund provided money for treatment and services for pregnant women and new mothers with substance abuse problems.
- Rhode Island—Infants considered at risk for exposure to a home environment where drugs are present can be removed from the home by the child protective service agency following a court order.
- Maryland and Minnesota—Services provided to at-risk families include family caseworkers and foster care for children.

Reporting Child Abuse

All parents and children have problems from time to time. Some of the signs of abuse listed earlier can be present without abuse. They serve as guides to use along with other physical and behavioral changes to point out when abuse must be considered as a possibility.

The reporting of suspected child abuse, as required by law in many states, has been criticized because it automatically triggers investigation and sometimes results in lawsuits. Accusations of child abuse in day-care centers have resulted in some highly publicized trials. While some of those cases have led to convictions, there is some criticism of required reporting laws because innocent people have sometimes been reported and investigated.

On the other hand, child and adolescent abuse, whether by parents, brothers or sisters, other family members, or others outside the family, can be reduced and prevented. And one key step in prevention is to report abuse. The failure to report allows further abuse that brings harm and injury. Abuse should be reported to law enforcement authorities, teachers, or social workers. There are also officials called child protective service workers whose job is to combat this problem. Reporting abuse can be difficult, especially if a friend has told you about it in confidence. Try to get your friend to talk to a counselor or teacher. That way you are helping without breaking your friend's confidence.

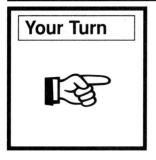

Your Turn

1. Brainstorm a list of the possible positive and negative effects of a state law requiring certain health, legal, education, or other professionals to report suspected child abuse. Who do you think should be required by law to report abuse? What can be done about the possibility of false reports that damage the reputation of the accused person? Do the benefits of reporting outweigh the costs?

2. Why do you think children often do not report abuse? What do you think schools, parents, or others in the community could do to educate children on the importance of reporting abuse?

3. You've been asked to watch two small children whose family just moved into your neighborhood. The children have some strange leg and arm bruises; one has a badly chipped tooth. Both cringe when you come near them. The house is fairly clean and the parents seem to care about their children. What do you do?

4. You go back to the same family for another child-care job. The younger child is fine, but the older one has lots of fresh bruises and is still afraid. What do you do now?

What Happens When Child Abuse Is Disclosed?

Disclosure of child abuse or incest can set off a chain of events including hospital visits, police interviews, and two possible kinds of court actions—a criminal proceeding focused on the acts of the offender and/or a child abuse and neglect civil proceeding.

As a result of court cases, the offender may be forced to leave the home or the victim may be temporarily removed from the home and placed with other relatives or in foster care. There is also the possibility that the victim will be permanently removed from the home. Commonly, the offender is placed on probation, and family members receive counseling and are under the supervision of a social worker. It's a tense, often chaotic time for families.

Support for Friends

For friends or professionals, the task of offering support to a child abuse victim is the same—work to ease the victim's trauma. A calm attitude, honesty, and an understanding discussion of the abuse and its effects are often most helpful.

Let the victim or family members choose when and how much they want to talk about it. Let them know you care and that you will be there through each step of the crisis. Direct them, when appropriate, to other sources of help (for example, counseling services in the community). The quality and amount of support can be critical to the victim and the victim's family as they try to build a healthy relationship.

Your support as a friend can make a big difference. Some ways to show your support include:

- Provide immediate help when there is a problem. Physical injury or a major conflict may significantly increase the chance that a child or teen will take serious action, such as running away. Often that can be more harmful than helpful.
- Ensure support and assistance to the abused by a social worker and friends or relatives. This may take the form of listening to problems or suggesting some resources to help with the problems.
- Suggest extended counseling for family members through mental health agencies or other professionals.

Teens and adults, as trained volunteers, can be effective in handling hotline calls on child abuse and other problems.

Your Turn

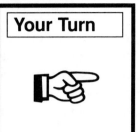

1. Suppose your friend comes to you for advice about a problem. She tells you that her brother's friend has been touching her inappropriately. What advice would you give her?
2. How could you convince a friend to go to the authorities and report abuse? What would make a person afraid to report?
3. Your high school friend confides information about the beatings she has received from her stepfather. She is a good student, but sometimes her school attendance is a problem. She tells you that several times, after severe beatings, she has been unable to come to school. Your friend tells you that all this started about two years ago when her stepfather lost his job. She does not wish to report it because she is afraid of her stepfather. What do you do?

Looking Back

You have been appointed to be the head of a youth service agency. One of the agency's main goals is to address the problem of child abuse. Make a list of all the services you think the agency should provide in order to have a major impact on child abuse. Which of your recommendations should receive top priority if funding is limited?

8

Acquaintance Rape

Words to Know

rape
acquaintance rape
date rape
perjury

Objectives

As a result of this chapter you should be able to:

- Define acquaintance rape

- Identify strategies to prevent acquaintance rape

- Describe ways that teens can help friends who are sexually assaulted

Use Your Experience	Have you heard the term *acquaintance rape*? Have you heard the term *date rape*? What do you think these terms mean?

What Is Acquaintance Rape?

Rape means sexual intercourse against the victim's will, typically with the use or threat of force. Some rapes are committed by strangers whom the victim has never seen before. Surveys show, however, that in at least one-half of all rapes, the victim knew the offender at least casually. **Acquaintance rape** frequently occurs as part of a social situation. **Date rape** is a sexual assault by a date, often a boyfriend or some other person with whom the victim has some sort of ongoing social relationship.

Some research suggests that in date rape situations, the assailant and the victim have frequently had at least three dates prior to the assault. In the most common situation, the victim and the date have a nice evening and then go somewhere isolated. Sometimes it's the date's apartment or another room away from the party. Whatever the situation, being forced to have sex against your will is rape. Some victims incorrectly assume that they cannot call what happened to them rape, if they knew and liked or had been personally involved with the offender.

Rape happens more often to teenage girls and young women than to women in any other age group or to men. Thirty percent of the rape victims in any year are 12 to 19 years old. Women ages 16 to 24 are more than three times as likely to be victims of rape than women in any other age group.

No one knows exactly how many people are victims of acquaintance rape each year. Many of these cases are never reported. Sometimes the victims do not consider the attack a rape, but the law makes no distinction: rape is rape, even if the attacker and the victim knew each other.

The Effects of Acquaintance Rape on Victims

Almost all rape victims feel anger, guilt, fear, and helplessness after the attack. They often mistakenly blame themselves, wondering if something they said, did, or wore provoked the assault.

Victims of acquaintance rape and date rape feel a special sense of shame and embarrassment. They knew, trusted, and possibly loved the offender, and these positive feelings were used to hurt them. How can victims trust their instincts again?

Victims who knew their rapists are less likely to report the crimes than those assaulted by strangers. Such victims may wish to protect the identity of the assailant and may even fear reprisals or worry that their account of the attack will not be believed. It is estimated that only 40 percent of all rapes or rape attempts were reported to the police in 1988.

The effects of acquaintance rape on the victim are often severe. The sense of violation and betrayal makes the victim feel guilty, depressed, fearful, and unable to place trust in others. The emotional injuries may make it difficult for a victim to have meaningful relationships in the future.

Victims of date rape may feel a sense of betrayal because they knew and trusted their attackers.

Your Turn

After returning from a party, a young woman and her boyfriend were alone in her apartment. She just wanted to relax and enjoy the music and the company. He began to kiss her and ask her to make love. When she said no, he got angry. She asked him to leave. Instead, he pushed her onto the bed and forced her to have sex. She felt disgusted and ashamed, as well as betrayed, and refused to go out with him again. She never reported the incident and still feels partly responsible.

1. Did the young woman have the right to refuse to make love? Why or why not?
2. What assumptions did the young man make about the young woman?
3. Did the young woman lead the young man to believe that this was what she wanted?
4. Should the boyfriend be held responsible for his behavior? Is it a crime?
5. What action, if any, should the young woman take? What action, if any, should the boyfriend take?
6. If you knew someone in this situation, what advice would you give her?
7. What attitudes encourage date or acquaintance rape? What can be done to change these attitudes?
8. List some of the consequences, for both the victim and society, of not reporting rape to the police.

In Your Community

1. Does your community have facilities or services for rape victims? Make a list of these services, and include police, rape crisis and mental health centers, hot lines, hospitals, and victim/witness and crisis intervention offices.
2. Does your community offer public education or any special preventive training services for rape? For acquaintance rape?
3. What are the rape statistics for your community? What percentage of these are acquaintance rapes? Date rapes?

Myths and Facts About Sexual Assault

Myth: Rape is motivated by sexual desire.

Fact: Rape is an act of violence. It is not motivated by sexual passion for the victim. It is an attempt to control and humiliate, using sex as the weapon. It is always wrong and a serious crime.

Myth: Victims invite rape by dressing seductively.

Fact: Victims do not cause rape. It can happen to anyone, young or old, no matter how he or she is dressed. Police believe that many rapists tend to prey on people who look frightened, appear to be easily intimidated, or seem to be daydreaming.

Myth: Most rapists rape only once.

Fact: Most rapists continue until caught. Since rape is one of the most underreported crimes, a rapist's criminal career can be long.

Myth: Only women and girls are raped.

Fact: Men and boys can also be victims of sexual assault. They can be raped by other males, for example. The male rape victim requires the same sort of support as the female victim.

Myth: The rapist is a healthy male out of control, provoked by a female.

Fact: The rapist attacks out of a desire for power, not out of attraction to the victim. The rapist usually selects circumstances and victims that will allow him to demonstrate power and control.

Myth: Women often make up stories of rape to get back at their boyfriends.

Fact: Women very rarely do this. If it happens, the person testifying to a lie in court can be charged and prosecuted for **perjury**.

Causes of Date Rape

There are appropriate ways to express affection for a date, but it is never permissible to touch the other person sexually if he or she objects, and it is never permissible to force sex. This is a criminal assault. No person has the right to force or demand the sexual activity of another.

Sometimes acquaintance rape occurs when people hold stereotypes about how males and females should act or at what point they think a dating relationship must include sex. Some males believe that they should be aggressive in order to force the female to give in. The man may believe that using force to impose his will on a female is acceptable behavior. The man or woman may feel that if the man pays for the evening's entertainment, this entitles him to have sex. It doesn't.

Lack of communication contributes to date rape situations. Poor communication between the two dating parties means each may not really know the other's expectations, sexual or otherwise.

The situation becomes more complicated if one person believes the other person is signaling for more involvement.

To communicate well, both parties must send clear, direct, and strong messages. Speak up about what you wish to do or avoid doing before any action is taken. This is the responsibility of both parties, as is thoughtful listening to the messages being sent.

How You Can Protect Yourself

- When you are going to date someone you don't know well, first check him or her out with friends. Plan to meet in a place where there are lots of people, or go out with friends. Avoid being alone in isolated or secluded places.
- Before you get into a situation you can't control, clearly and firmly let your date know your limits.
- Be prepared to find your own transportation home. Carry change for a phone call and enough cash for a taxi.

Do not go off alone with someone you've just met. Any time you sense that something is not quite right, or you feel uneasy, go someplace where there are other people.

- Don't get drunk or stoned. Drugs, including alcohol, decrease your ability to take care of yourself and make sensible decisions.
- Don't leave an event with someone you have just met.
- Don't ride in a car with someone you don't know and trust.
- If you think something's not quite right or you feel uneasy, go to where there are other people or tell your date to leave.
- Be assertive about how you feel and what you expect.
- If you've made your objections clear, stop worrying about the other person's feelings. Be rude, be forceful, be blunt if necessary.

What if it Happens to You?

- Call the police. Acquaintance rape is a crime, and it's more likely to occur again if it's not reported immediately. It may be more difficult to prosecute the person if you do not report immediately and preserve the evidence.
- Tell someone—your parents, a school counselor, the family doctor, or any adult you trust. Call your community's rape hot line or rape crisis center. It's important to talk about the incident and get counseling even though the memory is painful.
- Make sure you get medical attention for any injuries and are tested for venereal disease and pregnancy. Don't shower or bathe before going to the hospital, and don't destroy any of the clothing you were wearing. It may be important evidence.
- Remember, you didn't ask to be raped and are not to blame. Seek counseling. Share your feelings with other victims of sexual assault. Don't try to bury your emotions or minimize the trauma of a violent personal attack.

How to Help a Friend

Your support as a friend can make a big difference to someone who has been sexually assaulted. Following is a list* of things to keep in mind:

- Find a time and place to speak privately with your friend and listen to what he or she tells you. Let your friend talk; don't interrupt.
- Believe what your friend tells you. People rarely make up stories about sexual assault. Your friend has come to you feeling that you will believe the story. Your friend trusts you.

*Adapted from Victim Assistance Program, Sheriff's Department, Arapahoe County, Colorado.

- Let your friend know you care and you want to help. You may not know exactly what to do or what to say, but you can help find someone who does know. Help think of a trusted adult to tell, such as a school counselor, teacher, or rape crisis counselor.
- Sexual assault is wrong. Reassure your friend that the blame belongs on the offender.
- Encourage your friend to report the rape.
- Offer shelter if your friend needs a safe place to stay.

There are a number of community sources of help for rape victims, including those raped by someone they know. Sources include the police, rape crisis and mental health centers, hot lines, hospitals, and victim/witness and crisis intervention offices.

Young people can act as resources for their peers by providing information and advice on rape prevention.

Your Turn

You have volunteered to work for your community rape crisis hot line. A teenager calls in on Sunday evening because she thinks her date raped her on Saturday night. What advice would you give her?

Looking Back

Assume you are a writer for a popular magazine for teenagers in your city. Write a report explaining the problems of acquaintance rape and date rape and offering advice on methods for prevention. Why is this issue important for teenagers? What are the most important parts of this issue to explain to students? How could the information be most effectively presented? What resources from your community would you suggest to other teenagers?

9

Substance Abuse and Drug Trafficking

Words to Know

substance abuse
addiction
alcohol abuse
drug abuse
intravenous drugs
AIDS
paranoia
psychological
   dependency
inhalants
psychoactive
peer pressure
drug trafficking

Objectives

As a result of this chapter you should be able to:

■ Explain the problem of substance abuse in the United States, with special emphasis on teens

■ Identify the individual and community effects of substance abuse

■ Investigate your community's response to substance abuse

■ Discuss ways teens can avoid substance abuse

■ Discuss ways teens can help to prevent substance abuse

■ Explain the personal and legal consequences to an individual for selling illegal drugs

■ Identify how drug trafficking affects a community

■ Identify resources that can be used to reduce drug trafficking

Use Your Experience	Do you think there is a substance abuse problem in your community? If so, what substances are being abused? Why?

Have you heard about or witnessed the sale of illegal drugs in your neighborhood? If so, how have the neighborhood and its residents been affected? What other problems does the neighborhood experience?

What Is Substance Abuse?

The term **substance abuse** has come into general use in recent years. The word *substance* is used to describe all the kinds of chemicals—drugs, alcohol, and other materials—people have been found to abuse. Drugs are chemicals that can alter the way your mind and body work. When used properly, some drugs (such as prescribed medicines) can alter a sick person's body in a positive and healthy way.

Substance abuse describes the misuse of these chemicals. This is usually done to cause a temporary, artificial good feeling. Sometimes the misuse can result in **addiction**, which is a compulsion or overpowering urge to use a substance.

Addiction can be physical and/or psychological. Physical addiction means that a person's body has developed a need for the substance. Psychological addiction means that a person believes he or she must have the substance in order to function in the everyday world. This chapter examines the substances whose misuse or abuse can harm individuals and the community.

Alcohol Abuse

Alcohol is the most frequently abused substance in the United States. Although in most places use of alcohol by those over 21 years of age is legal, alcohol abuse causes many problems. These include car crashes caused by driving under the influence of alcohol, many work-related injuries, suicides, and a number of family-related problems.

What Is Drug Abuse?

Drug abuse is the wrongful use, misuse, or excessive use of any legal or illegal drug. Any use of an illegal substance is abuse. Cocaine is one example of an illegal drug. Medications supplied by the pharmacist to fill a doctor's prescription are legal, but they can be abused, too. Drug abuse can result in physical, mental, or emotional problems. It can also result in death.

Your Turn

What daily influences affect our views on substance abuse? Keep a log of ways in which you are exposed to information about drugs and alcohol in our society. For at least three days, log every contact that you have with substances that can be abused (including personal contact as well as media contact through popular songs, TV and radio advertising, jokes, and newspaper articles). Remember, we are talking about both legal and illegal substances, including such items as caffeine, nicotine, pills to keep you awake or make you sleep, and drugs to cure illnesses.

Use your log to discuss the following questions:

1. How often do we encounter references to drugs and alcohol in our daily lives?
2. How does our culture present the use of drugs and alcohol? As acceptable? Trendy? Appropriate? Illegal?
3. To which age groups are specific advertisements directed?
4. Do any of these references shape our attitudes toward drugs and alcohol? How?

How Substance Abuse Causes Problems

Substance abusers risk a lot of things when they get involved with drugs—their health, relationships, sometimes even their lives. The following are brief descriptions of some of the many problems that can arise from a person's use of drugs.

AIDS

People who illegally use **intravenous drugs** (drugs that are injected into the bloodstream) face a serious risk of contracting **AIDS** (Acquired Immune Deficiency Syndrome). It is known that the AIDS virus is transmitted from one person to another through sexual contact or the sharing of blood or other bodily fluids. When drug addicts share needles used by an infected person, they risk coming into contact with the infected person's blood. The Surgeon General of the United States has stated that needle sharing is a behavior that places a person at a high risk of contracting this deadly disease.

Emotional Problems

An extremely negative attitude, defensiveness, and **paranoia** (extreme suspiciousness) can result from the abuse of some drugs, including alcohol.

Legal Issues

Legal problems, such as a drug-related criminal record, can cost an abuser a job, a driver's license, many federal benefits, or even time in prison.

Family Relationships

Relationships are often strained when family members of drug abusers become angry, worried, or frightened by a loved one's use of drugs. The stress on family members can also cause them to become ill.

School Performance

Repeated use of some drugs causes the user often to be very confused or tired. This and other side effects can lead to increased absences from school, bad grades, memory lapses, difficulty in concentrating, increased tendency to get into fights, or reduced coordination in athletic activities.

Employment

It is often difficult for people who abuse drugs or alcohol to perform their duties in any job. It is also very difficult (sometimes impossible) for someone with a drug-related criminal record to work as a doctor, lawyer, teacher, police officer, engineer, or in any other job that requires a license or special insurance protection. With a record of drug abuse, people may be allowed to enlist in the military, but they may not be allowed their choice of duties.

Violence: Spouse and Child Abuse

Some people become more violent when under the influence of alcohol or other drugs. A high proportion of incidents of spouse and child abuse take place when the abuser is under the influence of these substances.

What Is Addiction?

Addiction, or dependency on drugs (including alcohol), is marked by a person's loss of control over his or her life as a result of using a certain substance.

All drugs can cause **psychological dependency**. This is the person's feeling that drugs are needed in order to cope with problems, to function better in life, or to feel different. This

Many teens know friends, classmates, or other teens with substance abuse problems.

false hope is difficult to overcome; the habit of taking the drug is strong. Just ask people who have tried to give up smoking cigarettes; the nicotine is out of their bodies in about three days, but the battle to give up the habit goes on and on. In fact, the psychological dependency on a drug is the hardest habit to break.

Physical Effects of Substance Abuse

Alcohol

Alcohol use is legal for adults in the United States. Alcohol consumption is so much a part of our society that it's easy to forget the harmful effects.

Many medical authorities believe that alcohol:

- Increases risk of liver damage
- Can cause birth defects
- Impairs coordination
- Destroys brain tissues
- Causes memory loss
- Causes personality disorders
- Is linked to several forms of cancer.

Alcohol use can also make it more difficult to think clearly or to perform physical tasks well (like driving a car). It can also cause miscommunication between people, heighten emotions, and result in violence. Many cases of spouse and child abuse involve alcohol.

Marijuana

Other than alcohol, marijuana is the illegal drug used most frequently by teens. Marijuana has been found to have many negative health effects.

Many medical authorities believe that marijuana:

- Decreases resistance to disease
- Obstructs air flow to the lungs
- Affects personality negatively
- Damages the reproductive systems of males and females
- Impairs physical development and coordination.

Cocaine

Cocaine use skyrocketed during most of the 1980s in the United States, among all age groups. The very temporary "high" that results from cocaine may give way to intense anxiety, depression, and confusion. Lethal overdoses of cocaine, either snorted or injected, increased.

Crack, a new form of cocaine, is cheap and easily available in some places, which makes it a special threat to the community. Often, crack overdoses result from the fact that a user requires a higher and higher dosage to equal the previous "high."

Inhalants

Inhalants are a diverse group of chemicals that produce **psychoactive** (mind-altering) vapors. Most of these chemicals are items that have a legitimate commercial purpose. Aerosol sprays, solvents, and synthetics are the principal inhalants used illegally.

Many medical authorities believe that inhalants:

- Disturb vision
- Impair judgment
- Reduce muscle and reflex control
- Cause brain damage
- Cause physical deterioration.

Alcohol, marijuana, cocaine, and inhalants are the substances most widely abused by young people. But other substances—heroin, hashish, barbiturates, and sedatives, to name a few—are also abused. They cause similar, or even more serious, damage to the abuser.

Trends in Substance Abuse Among Teens

The National Institute on Drug and Alcohol Abuse statistics for 1989 indicate that young people are decreasing their use of drugs. There has been an attitude shift among young people and a decline in the use of nearly all kinds of drugs. Alcohol use, however, remains high.

Still, young adults and adolescents are more likely than older adults to use illegal substances. The 1989 University of Michigan

Figure 1–Drug use rates among U.S. high school seniors, 1989

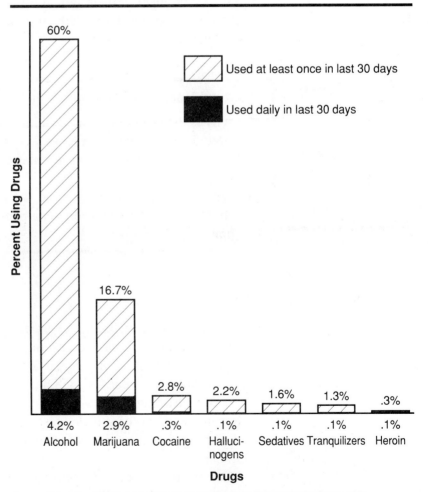

Source: University of Michigan Institute for Social Research, *Monitoring the Future,* 1989.

Nationwide Survey on the Life-styles and Values of Youth collected these statistics:

- More than 90 percent of high school seniors have used alcohol; 51 percent have tried an illicit drug.
- Seventeen percent of high school seniors reported using marijuana at least once in the 30 days prior to the survey.
- More than 10 percent of seniors had tried cocaine.
- Approximately 60 percent of seniors reported consuming alcohol in the 30 days prior to the survey.
- Many young people reported being "binge drinkers" who frequently consume five or more drinks in a row.

Many teens are aware of these problems among their friends, their classmates, and teens generally. Recent national opinion surveys show that teens see drug and alcohol use as the most significant problem of their age group. This may be contributing to the decline in the late 1980s and early 1990s in the use of some drugs among teens.

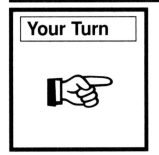

Your Turn

Look at Figure 1 and then answer the following questions.

1. Why is the alcohol use rate so high among teens?
2. How do the statistics in Figure 1 compare with what you think are the rates of substance abuse in your school? In your community?
3. Why would some teens become "binge drinkers"? What could be done to get these young people to stop this practice?

Looking at All the Costs

The total cost of substance abuse is difficult to estimate. However, it has been estimated that the cost of alcohol abuse in the United States was $85.8 billion in 1985. The estimate of the cost of drug abuse for the same year was $58.3 billion. These figures include the costs of treating abusers, of lost wages and work productivity due to abuse, of motor vehicle crashes, of extra law enforcement, and of programs designed to prevent or otherwise address the problem.

The cost to our society is enormous, but the cost to individuals is even greater. If someone we care about is being hurt by his or her use of drugs, it's a problem for us. We worry and try to help that person. That's time taken away from other activities. The stress we encounter can cause illness.

Your Turn

When a student comes to school under the influence of alcohol or drugs, it may seem that the student is the only victim, but is this true? Who else might be victims? What costs are involved in dealing with such a student? Brainstorm a list of costs as you see them.

In Your Community

1. What would be considered costs of substance abuse in your school district?
2. How much was spent on dealing with substance abuse in your school district last year?
3. What else could have been done with that money?

Decisions

No one starts out intending to become addicted to or dependent upon a substance. Many substances cause physical addiction. Others are so strongly addictive psychologically that their effects are equal, for practical purposes, to those of physically addictive substances. It is not possible for any person to tell ahead of time whether he or she will be able to use mind-altering substances and quit at will.

Addiction is a lifelong disease. People with addictions may learn to handle them, but the addiction itself never goes away.

Peer pressure—the influence of other people our age on each of us—can be difficult to handle at any age, but especially during the teen years. Teens are bombarded with physical, psychological, and emotional changes as part of growing up. Teens sometimes feel immense pressure to be accepted by their friends during this transitional and often confusing time.

The more you know about the negative consequences of alcohol and other drugs, the easier it will be to make intelligent decisions. It's wise to get all the facts about the possible costs and consequences

Peer pressure can be positive. Peers can encourage and support one another to be drug-free.

of drug and alcohol use. Investigate both the present and the future consequences. Look at the alternatives. It is a serious decision.

Once people have started using alcohol or other drugs, it becomes more and more difficult for them to say no. It may be clear to a friend or acquaintance that a person is a substance abuser, but it is usually difficult for the abuser to admit it. It is an individual's own choice to become involved with drugs, but friends and relatives can be good influences to prevent substance abuse.

Here are some things you can do as a friend or relative:

- Decide not to use drugs yourself, and explain that you make your own decisions based on what is right for you.
- Get involved and encourage your friends' involvement in fun, drug-free activities.
- Remind friends that the use of intravenous drugs places them at increased risk of getting AIDS.
- Learn more about the effects of alcohol and other drugs and share this information.
- Remind friends that buying or possessing alcohol, marijuana, cocaine, and most other drugs is against the law.

Your Turn

1. What do you think of the "Just Say No" campaign? Is it working? What would it take to get a project like that started in your school?
2. Role-play the following situation:

   You are at a party with lots of people, some of whom you know. Someone passes a joint of marijuana around. You have decided that you don't want to smoke it. Come up with some ways of responding or acting toward your friends that will allow you to do what you want (not smoke). You may have a friend with you who also doesn't want to smoke. How do you think others would respond to your ways of dealing with this situation?

Some Signs of Abuse

It is important to recognize signs that someone is in trouble because of the use of alcohol or other drugs. The following is a list of *possible* indicators of an abuse problem. These may not necessarily indicate a drug problem, but a person who has many of these symptoms is troubled by something and needs your help.

Increased Focus on Alcohol or Other Drugs

- Talking about and planning for the next use
- Talking about buying drugs or alcohol
- Increasing the frequency of usage or the amount used (was weekly, is now daily)

Physical Evidence

- Drug paraphernalia: papers, pipes, needles, razor blades
- Bottles or cans of alcohol in car or locker
- Possession of large, unexplained amounts of money

Changes in Health or Appearance

- Drastic increase or decrease in weight
- Change in personal habits (for example, a neat person is suddenly very sloppy)
- Slurred or incoherent speech

Changes in Personality and Mood

- Depressions, withdrawal from others
- Disorientation or inability to concentrate
- Secretiveness or paranoia

Changes in Friendships

- Dropping nonusing friends for friends who use drugs
- Suspicious-sounding phone calls
- Secretive friends
- Friends expressing concern about the person's use

Changes in Performance in School, Work, and Activities

- Drop in grades
- Absenteeism, tardiness
- Dropping out of previously liked activities, such as sports or band

Decline in Family Relationships

- Family shows concern or anger over person's behavior
- Person withdraws from family
- Person lies to or steals from family
- Chronic disregard for family rules

Reliance on Excuses

- Blames everyone and everything, except himself or herself, for life's problems
- Denies that alcohol or other drug use could be the cause of his or her problems

One or even several of these are not conclusive proof of drug use. Evaluate changes in view of your long-term knowledge of the individual. Drug users hide signs of use, and all young people occasionally exhibit some of these emotional symptoms.

*How to Talk to a Friend Who's in Trouble with Alcohol or Other Drugs**

1. Plan ahead what you want to say and how you want to say it.
2. Pick a quiet and private time to talk with your friend.

3. Don't try to talk to your friend about the problem when the friend is drunk or high.
4. Use a calm voice.
5. Let your friend know that you care.
6. Describe what you're concerned about and how you feel about it. Be specific. (Example: "I get scared for you when you sneak out to smoke pot during lunch. I'm afraid you're going to get into more trouble.")
7. Let your friend know what you like—and what you don't like—about the friend's behavior when straight and when high or drunk. (Example: "When you're straight, you're easygoing and friendly. When you're drinking, you get in fights easily, and that's not fun to be around.")
8. Don't get into an argument. If one gets started, you can say, "I'm not going to argue with you. I just wanted you to know why I'm concerned about you."
9. Ask if there's anything you can do to help. Offer suggestions. (Example: "I'll go with you if you want to go talk to the school counselor.")
10. Don't expect your friend to like what you're saying. But remember, the more people share their concerns, the more likely it is your friend may take a look at his or her behavior. (Example: "You're the fourth person who has said they are worried about my use of pot. Maybe I should go talk to somebody and see what they think.")
11. Remember: It's not your job to get people to stop taking drugs or drinking alcohol. You can talk to them and care about them, but only they can decide to stop.
12. Take care of yourself. Talk about the situation with someone who knows about alcohol and drug abuse.

Teens and Substance Abuse Prevention

If you are concerned about drug use by a number of your classmates and friends, remember there are things teens can do to help change the situation. Often, what is needed is one person who has the goal of a drug-free school or neighborhood and is willing to work to make it a reality. The key is to gather together other students or neighbors with the same goal and share in the work and in fun activities.

*Adapted from Prevention and Intervention Center for Alcohol and Drug Abuse, *Reason and Responsibility: A Curriculum for Alcohol and Other Drug Abuse Prevention* (1985). Used with permission.

School-based groups organized to prevent drug use have become involved in a number of different recreational, educational, and community service projects. The following are some of the activities organized by teens around the country to help their schools and communities prevent drug use:

- Sports events or other drug-free recreational activities
- Community service projects such as schoolyard or park cleanups or visits to the elderly
- Educational assemblies
- Training sessions for teens who teach younger kids about the dangers of drug use
- Student leadership training.

State and Federal Drug Laws

There are both state and federal laws concerning drugs. These laws usually define legal and illegal substances, forbid specific behavior (possession, use, sales), and provide penalties for conviction.

Federal Laws

At the federal level, the Drug Enforcement Administration and the Food and Drug Administration decide whether drugs are illegal or not. In general, the more potential a drug has for abuse, the stricter the control required by the federal government.

State Laws

State laws regarding drug abuse vary. The sample state statute in Figure 2 is typical. It has been put into diagram form to make it easier to read. Note the careful language as you read the statute. The first sections of the statute outline the behavior that is forbidden. The next sections outline the potential sentences.

Penalties

Federal laws and most state laws now carry harsher penalties. Those who sell drugs or possess large amounts with intent to sell often face mandatory jail terms even for their first offense. Under federal law and in some states, those found guilty of being major drug traffickers may face a sentence of "life without parole." Some states even treat simple possession of small amounts of certain types of drugs as felonies.

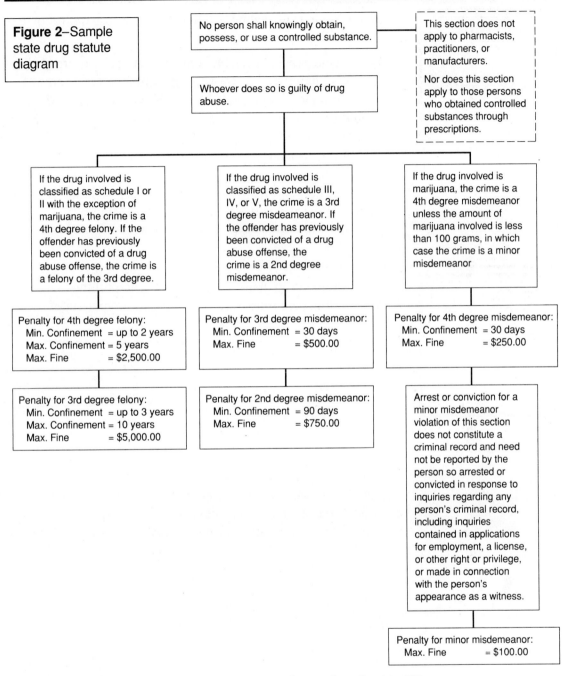

Figure 2–Sample state drug statute diagram

No person shall knowingly obtain, possess, or use a controlled substance.

This section does not apply to pharmacists, practitioners, or manufacturers.

Nor does this section apply to those persons who obtained controlled substances through prescriptions.

Whoever does so is guilty of drug abuse.

If the drug involved is classified as schedule I or II with the exception of marijuana, the crime is a 4th degree felony. If the offender has previously been convicted of a drug abuse offense, the crime is a felony of the 3rd degree.

If the drug involved is classified as schedule III, IV, or V, the crime is a 3rd degree misdeameanor. If the offender has previously been convicted of a drug abuse offense, the crime is a 2nd degree misdemeanor.

If the drug involved is marijuana, the crime is a 4th degree misdemeanor unless the amount of marijuana involved is less than 100 grams, in which case the crime is a minor misdemeanor

Penalty for 4th degree felony:
Min. Confinement = up to 2 years
Max. Confinement = 5 years
Max. Fine = $2,500.00

Penalty for 3rd degree misdemeanor:
Min. Confinement = 30 days
Max. Fine = $500.00

Penalty for 4th degree misdemeanor:
Min. Confinement = 30 days
Max. Fine = $250.00

Penalty for 3rd degree felony:
Min. Confinement = up to 3 years
Max. Confinement = 10 years
Max. Fine = $5,000.00

Penalty for 2nd degree misdemeanor:
Min. Confinement = 90 days
Max. Fine = $750.00

Arrest or conviction for a minor misdemeanor violation of this section does not constitute a criminal record and need not be reported by the person so arrested or convicted in response to inquiries regarding any person's criminal record, including inquiries contained in applications for employment, a license, or other right or privilege, or made in connection with the person's appearance as a witness.

Penalty for minor misdemeanor:
Max. Fine = $100.00

Source: Adapted from Cleveland-Marshall College of Law, Street Law Program, *Street Chemistry*, 1983.

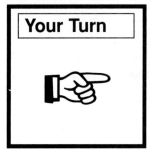

Your Turn

Use the sample state statute in Figure 2 to discuss the following situations:

1. Steve, who grew marijuana in his apartment, was arrested for and convicted of possessing an estimated 400 grams of the controlled substance. What can Steve's penalty be? Would the penalty differ if he were arrested and convicted for possessing 90 grams of marijuana?
2. Teresa is arrested with six ounces of cocaine (schedule 1 drug) in her purse. She has never been arrested for drug use or possession before. What can her penalty be if she is found guilty? What if this were Teresa's second offense?

In Your Community

1. What do the drug abuse laws in your state prohibit?
2. Which drugs are most strictly controlled in your state? Which are least controlled?

Lake Place

"You would be crazy to walk the streets then."

That is how one young mother, a resident of an impoverished neighborhood in a major city, describes the situation when asked how often she goes out at night. (This is a true story, but the name of the neighborhood has been changed.)

Residents, community leaders, and police have described Lake Place as a 24-hour-a-day crack cocaine market. Police cruisers routinely patrol the three elementary schools and rows of homes and apartment buildings in the area. But they know the drug dealers use children as lookouts to warn the dealers to scatter before anyone can be arrested. Residents say dealing begins again as soon as the police are out of sight.

The young mother and many other residents are frightened nightly by the sounds of gunfire from youths huddled on street corners and in buildings. Parents rush their children home after school and often keep them indoors, fearing for their safety amid the violence. Older teens and adults often do not go out at night, afraid they will be caught in a shooting war between rival drug-selling gangs. One neighbor even commented that the area was like the old Wild West. One teen, expressing the way a lot of teens feel, commented, "Don't call it Lake Place. Call it Death Valley."

The physical evidence of trouble is everywhere. The lawns and the vacant lots are littered with debris, some apartment doors have bullet holes in them, and the walls of several buildings are covered with graffiti. The courtyard of a building, scene of a drug-related shooting, is roped off with yellow police tape. One teen said that police may as well leave the tape up because they're sure to need it again soon.

Obviously, neither the residents nor neighborhood groups are happy about this situation. People are reluctant to come to Lake Place for their regular legitimate business. "Sometimes my mother says I don't want to come see her that much anymore because I don't love her," one middle-aged woman said, staring grimly up the street toward two teen lookouts. "But I really do love her. It's just that I'm so scared here." The drug-selling youths and the violence have nearly everyone scared and unsure of what to do to solve the problem.

Your Turn

1. In addition to drug trafficking, what other problems does Lake Place have?
2. Who do you think is responsible for the drug-trafficking problem in Lake Place? Below is a list of ten groups of people. Rank the groups from 1 to 10 in order of responsibility for the problems in Lake Place, beginning with 1 for the group most responsible. Discuss the reasons for your rankings. Are there any other groups that should be held responsible that are not listed here? Which ones are they?

   _____   The drug dealers
   _____   The people who supply the dealers with drugs
   _____   Lake Place residents who buy drugs
   _____   People from other areas who buy drugs in Lake Place
   _____   The police
   _____   The city government
   _____   Lake Place residents who witness drug sales but do not report the incidents to police
   _____   Lake Place teens not involved in drugs
   _____   The media (newspapers, radio, TV)
   _____   Parents of Lake Place youth

What Is Drug Trafficking?

Drug use is one of our nation's major problems. Closely tied to it is the problem of drug sales. Almost all drug users purchase their drugs from someone else or take drugs from the supply they sell to others.

Drug trafficking is the term used to describe the unlawful sale of substances such as marijuana, cocaine, heroin, or other illegal drugs. The people who traffic in these drugs are called drug dealers. Alcohol is a legal drug for people over 21 years of age. The other drugs mentioned in this paragraph are not legal for anyone.

How Does Drug Trafficking Affect Teens?

Teens who become involved in drug trafficking do so for any number of reasons, including money and peer pressure. Teens who get involved for the money often may have legal jobs that they feel do not pay enough or do not offer opportunities for advancement. As in the case of substance abuse, the pressure to get involved in drug sales can be very strong, especially in areas where gang activity is based on drug trafficking.

Some youth who have low self-esteem and are not hopeful about their future may have a difficult time recognizing that they have choices that do not involve trafficking. Youth who choose to become traffickers often do so because they believe it is an exciting way to make a lot of money quickly.

The considerable dangers and risks to teens involved in trafficking include:

- Death or serious injury—Young people who get involved in trafficking are much more likely to be murder victims or suffer serious gunshot wounds than uninvolved youth.
- Incarceration—A significant number of young people in secure juvenile justice institutions are there for drug trafficking. Adult traffickers often get youth to work for them by falsely promising that they will not be sent to jail because they are juveniles.

One 1988 study of 15- to 17-year-old males in a major U.S. city found that the great majority were not involved in using or selling drugs. The youth who were involved in using or selling drugs were much less likely to have completed high school than those not involved. Those who were drug users or drug sellers were also more than twice as likely as nonusers and nonsellers to have repeated a grade in school. The study concluded that youth who use or sell drugs have problems with school, family, criminal involvement, and low self-esteem.

The study also provided the following statistics about youth who sold drugs in a major U.S. city:

- One out of every six of the 15- to 16-year-olds and almost one out of every three of the 16- to 17 year-olds admitted to having sold drugs in the previous year. Fifty-five percent of those who admitted to selling drugs said they had done so at least five times.
- Sixty-two percent of the drug sellers believed their actions would eventually get them seriously injured or killed.
- Eighty-eight percent also admitted to committing violent or property crime in the previous year.
- Eighty percent did not admire people who sell drugs.

In contrast to rumors and stereotypes, many drug dealers don't make more money than other people. Someone trained for a legitimate job gets the acceptance and respect of society, much less risk, and the potential for a long and rewarding career that drug dealing cannot offer. After a few years' experience, a number of jobs provide equal or better pay than that of the average drug dealer. These positions are held by teachers, plumbers, store managers, computer programmers, lawyers, postal workers, and police officers, among others.

Your Turn

1. Name three careers you have considered for yourself. What factors determine the type of job you might want? What kinds of skills do you think you might need?
2. Compare the professions of a doctor, teacher, plumber, drug trafficker, firefighter, major league baseball player, race-car driver, and construction worker in terms of the following factors: difficulty, number of hours worked, training and education, special talent needed, responsibility, and risk. How much of each factor do the different jobs involve?

The Risks and Realities of Drug Trafficking

The risk and competition involved in the sale of illegal drugs breed a cycle of violence and crime. As part of the job, drug dealers and the people who work for them carry a lot of cash and often a gun to protect themselves and their money. While fighting for control over territory with other dealers, they often get involved in shooting wars during which they injure or kill each other or innocent bystanders.

In one major U.S. city, police estimated that 58 percent of the murders in 1988 were drug-related. In most of those cases, the victim was a young man killed near his home in the area of a drug sale.

A 1990 study revealed that out of 100 drug dealers in the District of Columbia, one was killed, 11 were seriously injured, and 22 were convicted of a crime in that single year. Over several years, the chances of being killed, injured seriously, or imprisoned increase significantly.

The study indicated that drug dealing is not a quick and exciting path to a better life. Some drug dealers realize this and get out of the business before they are injured, killed, or imprisoned.

Your Turn

Role-play a discussion between 14-year-old Tiffany and her 16-year-old brother Tony. Tiffany knows that Tony is dealing cocaine to other teens in the neighborhood and that he's planning to buy a gun. Tiffany is concerned about her brother. Tony tells her he'll be fine once he has the gun to protect himself.

1. What arguments does Tiffany make? What arguments does Tony make?
2. Which arguments are most convincing? Why?

How Do Illegal Drugs and Trafficking Relate to Other Crime?

Drug users and many who deal drugs to support their habits get involved in violent and property crime as a way to get money to pay for the drugs. A history of drug use is nearly twice as common among people now in prison as it is for the general population. In addition, some people's judgment is altered by some of these drugs, which are now more powerful than ever before. Certain drugs have been said to cause criminal behavior in some individuals.

In addition to promoting the use of drugs and helping people to become addicted in order to get more business, drug traffickers in the United States have become a major crime problem in several other ways.

The traffickers use the illegal profits to buy more illegal drugs and/or weapons or to invest in legal businesses. The weapons are bought to protect the trafficker. Investments are made in legal businesses in an effort to hide the traffickers' money from government authorities. Tracing money from these businesses to a particular dealer is very difficult and time-consuming for law enforcement officers.

Competition for customers among drug traffickers is very intense because of the high dollar value of the drugs. The violent struggles between heavily armed rival traffickers attempting to protect their territory or gain new territory sometimes result in murder.

When Drug Traffickers Get Caught

Drug traffickers face a substantial risk of death or serious injury. In addition, they also have to serve time in prison after they are caught and convicted of drug-trafficking offenses. Adults who were convicted of drug trafficking under federal laws from 1987 to 1990 received an average sentence of six years in prison.

Juveniles are also arrested for drug-trafficking offenses. The Federal Bureau of Investigation's (FBI's) annual *Uniform Crime Report* (UCR) includes statistics on the number of juveniles arrested for drug abuse violations, including trafficking. More than 90,000 teens were arrested for such offenses in 1989. The UCR data also show a 12 percent increase in the number of juveniles arrested for drug abuse violations from 1985 to 1989. There was a disturbing 68 percent increase in the number of youths under 10 years of age arrested for these offenses during the same four-year period. In one major U.S. city, the number of juveniles arrested for drug trafficking increased from 58 to 1,550 between the years 1981 and 1988.

Juveniles from all types of areas are arrested. In 1989, 77,539 juveniles from urban areas were arrested for drug abuse violations. That is a 10 percent increase over the figures for 1988. More than 9,700 juveniles living in suburban counties were arrested for drug abuse violations in 1989, an 18.3 percent increase over 1988.

Under California law, as one example, tough minimum criminal sentences are imposed for trafficking in controlled substances such as cocaine, heroin, and other narcotics:

- Five to nine years in state prison for distribution of narcotics on school grounds by an adult—up to five more years can be added if the juvenile to whom the drugs are sold is more than four years younger than the adult offender.
- Three to nine years in state prison for sale or distribution of drugs in a public park by an adult.

Figure 3–Female arrestees testing positive for drug use, 1989

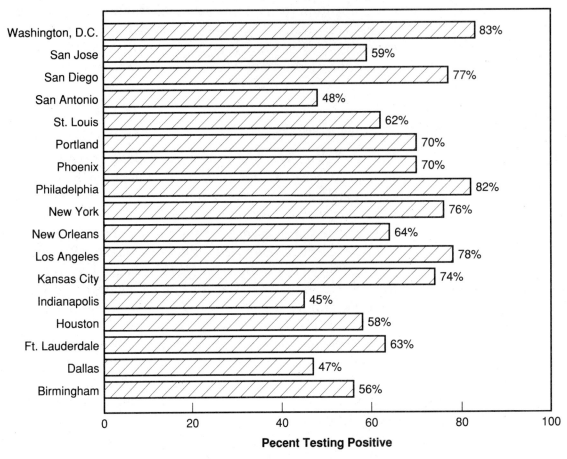

Souce: National Institute of Justice, *Drug Use Forecasting Reports,* 1989.

- Three to seven years in state prison for an adult·who hires a juvenile to sell or transport drugs—up to three more years can be added if the juvenile is more than four years younger than the adult offender.
- Juveniles who enlist other juveniles to sell or transport drugs are punished by serving time in state prison.

Special conditions of the California law allow for significant additions to sentences for trafficking. These include up to three more years for prior convictions on the same offense, from three to 15 additional years for convictions involving especially large amounts of controlled substances, and up to four more years for unlawful possession of a controlled substance and a firearm.

Figure 4–Male arrestees testing positive for drug use, 1989

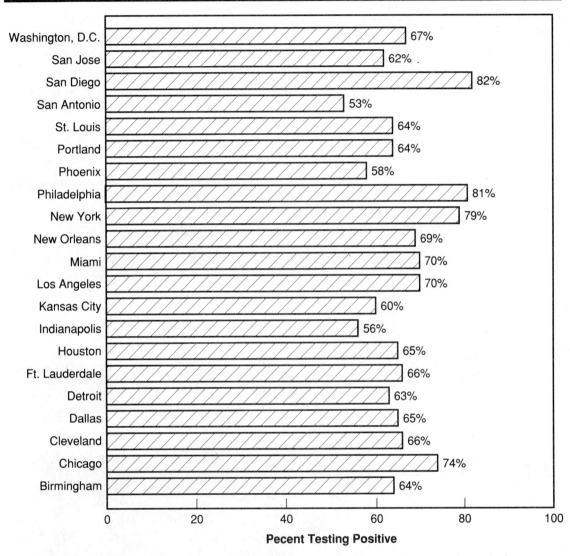

Souce: National Institute of Justice, *Drug Use Forecasting Reports*, 1989.

Your Turn

1. You are a state legislator. What criminal penalties for drug trafficking would you want to see written into the law? Under what conditions would you impose the longest sentences?
2. Take note of Figures 3 and 4. They represent the 1989 results of an ongoing federal "Drug Use Forecasting" program involving voluntary drug testing among a sample of arrestees

in 22 major cities. Those tested were generally persons arrested for crimes other than the sale or possession of drugs. Arrestees were invited to provide anonymous, voluntary urine samples for analysis. Tests were conducted for cocaine, opiates, marijuana, PCP, methadone, valium, methaqualone, Darvon, barbiturates, and amphetamines. The tests detect most drugs used up to two to three days prior to the test. Marijuana and PCP are sometimes detected up to several weeks after their use.

Why do you think the results might vary so much from city to city? What factors do you think might account for the variations among cities and between sexes?

How Does Drug Trafficking Affect the Community?

There is a very real and frightening cost to the community in the lives lost or individuals severely injured as a result of crimes related to drug trafficking. In addition, there are other important costs to the community.

Substance abuse, drug trafficking, and other crime have negative effects of the community. They lead to violence and fear, which make life unpleasant for everyone.

- The lives of residents are restricted. They don't go out at night and sometimes even in the daytime because they are fearful. Some residents move out of the neighborhood.
- Legitimate businesses shut down because the owners fear the violence and theft inspired by drug trafficking. This results in a loss of jobs.
- Apartments and other buildings are not maintained because the owners are unable to keep up with the cost of replacing or repairing doors, walls, or other items damaged by gunshots, vandalism, or graffiti.
- Residents and businesses lose money and possessions in burglaries and other crimes committed by addicts and dealers.
- The city has to spend much more money than it planned on extra police patrols and crime investigations in the area. The investigations are long and difficult because residents who are witnesses fear the revenge of dealers and do not want to testify.
- Vacant lots or buildings are not developed because the owners do not think of the community as a safe place to do business.
- Other neighborhood problems get worse as drug trafficking causes further community decline.

Some communities have made significant efforts to save their neighborhoods from deteriorating due to drug-related and other crime. Through community crime prevention programs, people work together to develop safer and more pleasant living conditions.

In Your Community

What kinds of community or school-based programs exist in your area to educate teens about the dangerous realities of drugs and drug trafficking in your community?

Looking Back

Imagine you are the teen adviser to the local neighborhood commission, which is made up of citizens and local government and law enforcement officials. Your community is in the same city as the Lake Place neighborhood described at the beginning of the section on drug trafficking. The commission has heard about the problems Lake Place has had with drug trafficking, shootings, and other crime and does not want them to happen in its own area.

Because the commission knows that many of the drug dealers on the streets are teens or young people, they have asked for your advice.

Consider the economic, social, and physical conditions that may have contributed to the drug trafficking and other problems in Lake Place and the extent to which your neighborhood experiences the same conditions.

List the people and other resources that need to be brought together to address these conditions and issues in your neighborhood. Use that list to develop five recommendations you would present to the commission about the use of these resources.

10

Drunk Driving

Words to Know

intoxicated
drunk
impaired
psychological
   intoxication
blood alcohol
   concentration
revocation
implied consent law
compensated

Objectives

As a result of this chapter you should be able to:

- Define the crime of driving while under the influence of alcohol

- Discuss the human and legal consequences of drunk driving

- Explain how alcohol affects the user's body, behavior, and driving ability

- Identify techniques you can use to avoid the dangers of drunk driving

- Recommend strategies and resources that can be used in your school and the community to combat drunk driving

Use Your Experience	Have you ever been with anyone who was driving while **intoxicated**? Do you know anyone who has been injured or killed in an automobile crash caused by drunk driving? What were the circumstances of the crash? What happened to those who were involved in the crash?

When Alcohol Kills*

The following is an excerpt:

Americans have a philosophy of life that goes something like this: "It can't happen to me; it's always the other guy that things happen to." In some ways that outlook is good because if we were always worried about what was going to happen, we would be paralyzed and unable to accomplish much. As a naval aviator, I was no different; I believed it was always going to be the other pilot who crashed and burned. And as a parent, I believed it was always the other parents' kid who was going to be involved in a fatal automobile crash.

But on January 1, 1982, an event happened that was to change my philosophy, my life, and the life of my family.

At about 9:30 P.M. on December 31, 1981, our youngest daughter Susan came into the den to kiss us good-bye before leaving for a New Year's Eve party at the home of a schoolmate. Even though she was 19 years old, she asked what her curfew was and I told her, "1:00 A.M." She said, "Dad, it's such a special night, the last New Year's together with all my school friends." She was a senior in high school, a responsible teenager, a good driver, vice-president of her senior class, and a member of the Catholic Youth Organization executive board and the area youth encounter group. So I gave in and stretched the curfew to 1:30 A.M. We didn't realize then how final it really was to be.

My wife, my mother, and I had a quiet New Year's at home and went to bed just after 1 A.M. At approximately 1:40 A.M., while sitting in bed waiting for Susan to come home, we received a phone call from the mother at the party that Susan had attended. She asked if Susan was home and when I told her "no," she said that there had been an accident (we now call it a crash) on the main street that runs through our subdivision. We hurriedly dressed and drove down to the crash site, less than a mile from our house.

*Louis L. Herzog and Charles A. Hurley, "When Alcohol Kills." Taken from "A Generation At Risk," a documentary aired on public television and published as a book under the same title.

We parked at the top of the hill and I asked the police officer if it was Susan. He said, "Yes." I asked if she was alive. He said, "No."

I still find it impossible to explain what went through my mind and how I felt, but I do remember walking over to the crushed VW Beetle and throwing my keys at it and watching the key ring break apart. The keys flew in all directions and I began crying (I've shed a lot of tears since then). We went home and sat there, thinking it was a bad dream and we'd wake up and it would all go away, but it didn't.

At 8 A.M., the police officer came over and said, "Mr. Herzog, I'm sorry but I'll have to ask you to come with me to the morgue and identify Susan's body." When I saw her on the gurney, I realized that it wasn't a bad dream and that for the rest of my life I'd have to live with the fact that she had been killed.

We didn't have all the facts then, but as the police and our family began to investigate, we found a trail of irresponsible actions. If only one of the persons involved that night had acted *responsibly*, and broken the chain of events, Susan might be alive today.

In fact, if all of us had acted responsibly last year, perhaps some of the 22,500 people who died as a result of drunk-driving crashes might be alive today. Certainly, if all of us act more responsibly now and in the future, an additional 22,500 people may not have to die this year as well. More importantly, if we don't begin this process now, we will never make any additional progress toward stopping the carnage on the road, and none of our families will be immune.

Your Turn

Assume you are part of the police investigation team working on this case. During the investigation you uncover the following facts:

a. It was a two-car accident. Susan's car was struck by a vehicle that crossed the center line and hit her head on.

b. The vehicle that struck Susan's was driven by a male under 21 years of age who survived the crash and who was unquestionably **drunk**. Susan was neither drunk nor **impaired** in her driving.

c. At the party the drunk driver attended, the host, who was under 21 years of age, gave each couple a bottle of champagne he had purchased.

d. The parents of the host, who were upstairs at the time, allowed the alcohol to be served.

e. The intoxicated driver had also purchased alcohol at two supermarkets. In one store, he had used someone else's identification; the other store did not request identification.

You and the rest of the investigation team have been asked to decide who is responsible for the crash. First, make a list of all the people who might be in some way responsible. Note the reasons for any legal responsibility. After you have completed your list, decide where you think the final responsibility should fall, legally and morally.

How Does Drunk Driving Relate to Teens?

Young people—as drivers or as passengers—are at a higher risk than adults of being injured or killed in alcohol-related crashes. In fact, alcohol-related traffic crashes are the leading killers of young people in America.

The facts speak for themselves:

- About half of all highway deaths involve alcohol. Translated into numbers, this means 22,500 people a year (432 a week) die in alcohol-related crashes. That's one alcohol-related fatality every 23 minutes. Almost 4,000 of the fatalities each year are teens.
- In addition, some 345,000 people (over 100,000 of them teens) were injured in alcohol-related crashes in 1989.
- In 1989, 10 percent of the teens fatally injured in alcohol-related crashes were *not* passengers or drivers in motor vehicles. This means that these teens were probably pedestrians or bicyclists.

Why Are Teens So Frequently Involved?

There are many reasons why drunk driving so frequently involves teens:

- Alcohol is the drug most widely used and abused by teens. Some 4.6 million teens in the United States are known to have problems with alcohol. Although the drinking age in every state and the District of Columbia is 21, results of a 1989 University of Michigan survey showed that 60 percent of high school seniors had consumed alcohol in the past month and a third of them had consumed five or more drinks in a row within the previous two weeks.

- In general, teens weigh less than adults. The same amount of alcohol under similar circumstances will have a greater effect on a lighter-weight person than on a heavier person.
- Because teens are relatively inexperienced with alcohol, they often develop **psychological intoxication**, which means they feel and act more intoxicated than their **blood alcohol concentration** levels would suggest.
- Teens are less experienced drivers. Because driving is relatively new to teens, it requires more conscious effort by them. Thus, their performance is likely to deteriorate more rapidly from the effects of alcohol.

Going to an amusement park is one of many activities teens can enjoy without alcohol or other drugs.

- Teen auto crashes are most likely to occur at times when teens are also most likely to abuse alcohol: at night, on weekends, and with peers. Speeding is often a factor in these crashes, which frequently involve a single car.
- People in this age group are least likely to believe that seat belts should always be used. Drinking often reduces whatever urge exists to buckle up.

Aside from the tragic loss of life, drunk driving has economic costs that affect us all. Alcohol-related crashes cause insurance rates to soar, mostly for the responsible party but also for those who follow the law and their common sense. In some cases, insurance policies of convicted drunk drivers may be canceled. There are other significant costs to individuals and society, including medical expenses and time missed from work.

Your Turn

1. Why do you think so many single-car accidents involve drunk drivers?
2. Give three reasons why car crashes can be caused by teens who consume low levels of alcohol.

The Legal Drinking Age

Alcohol is controlled by law in each of the 50 states and the District of Columbia. The problem of teenage drunk driving must be considered in connection with the legal drinking age of 21. During the 1980s, the public's attention was drawn to alcohol and alcohol-related problems. All state legislatures that had not already done so raised their states' legal drinking age to 21.

The fact that all states and the District of Columbia have raised the legal drinking age to 21 means that teens who drive drunk violate two laws: drinking under age and driving under the influence. Many states have extended the definition of driving under the influence to include illegal drugs such as cocaine and marijuana. Some state laws also include legal drugs or medications that interfere with a person's ability to drive. Drugged-driving charges can be imposed in addition to charges of illegal drug use and drug possession. As of 1991, 15 states also had laws allowing the driver's licenses of those under 18 to be revoked or suspended for possession of alcohol. In these states the drivers can lose their licenses whether or not the possession is related to or has affected their driving.

Many people believe that the legal drinking age of 21 has been justified by the dramatic reduction in the number of deaths due to drunk driving that followed its enactment. Others feel that these laws are unfair to those ages 18 to 21 because they conflict with the age for adult rights, such as voting.

Statistics show that the proportion of 16- to 20-year-old intoxicated drivers involved in fatal crashes dropped by 40 percent from 1982 to 1989. The National Highway Traffic Safety Administration believes that this and other changes in law were effective in reducing traffic fatalities involving drivers of all age groups by 13 percent, a dramatic saving of over 10,000 lives in the 1982–89 period.

In a related area, parents or other adults who supervise parties where alcohol is consumed by teens run the risk of being held responsible if any injury or accident results. Adults who provide alcohol to minors can be charged, convicted, and fined or imprisoned.

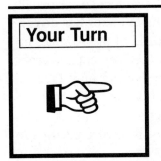

Your Turn

1. What are the arguments for and against a legal drinking age of 21?
2. If you were a member of a state legislature, where would you set the minimum age for drinking?
3. Does your state have any law against drugged driving?
4 How does the law in your state handle the problem of a drunk boat operator? What other vehicles are covered under your state's law?

How Does the Law Treat Drunk Driving?

The term *drunk* is used in general conversation to refer to the condition of someone whose behavior has been changed or impaired by the consumption of alcohol. Legally, someone is drunk if his or her blood alcohol concentration (BAC) is above a certain level. (See Figure 1.)

The BAC describes the percentage in the bloodstream of the chemical compound alcohol, a mind-altering drug. A person's BAC can be determined through breath, urine, or blood samples. A BAC of 0.10 percent means that out of 1,000 units of blood, 10 units are alcohol. Tests have shown that thought processes, physical reactions, coordination, and vision are affected in various degrees by the level of alcohol in the bloodstream. The probability of an alcohol-related crash begins to increase significantly at 0.05 percent blood alcohol concentration—which is half the legal limit in most states.

Every state in the country has set BAC limits for driving while intoxicated (DWI) or driving under the influence (DUI). According to the laws in the great majority of states, a person with a BAC of 0.10 percent is considered to be intoxicated. As of the beginning of 1991, a few state legislatures introduced legislation to lower the BAC level used to define intoxication to 0.08 percent.

The penalties a driver may face for DWI or DUI include the following:

- License suspension
- License **revocation** (cancellation)
- Jail sentence
- Fine
- Mandatory enrollment in DWI school
- Community service.

Generally, any combination of penalties may be imposed by the court. A repeat offender is likely to receive a stiffer penalty and in many states will automatically have his or her driver's license suspended. As of January 1, 1990, 45 of the 50 states had established laws defining a BAC level of 0.10 percent as a crime. People convicted of alcohol-impaired driving may face jail sentences even for first offenses in all but two states.

A driver who has been stopped may choose not to take a test for DWI. However, most states have an **implied consent law**.

Figure 1–Laws on blood alcohol concentration levels in 44 states, 1990	**BAC Level**	**Status in Law**
	0.05% or less	This is evidence of not being under the influence of alcohol. Driving ability may be diminished but alcohol content alone does not provide cause for a DWI conviction.
	0.06%–0.09%	There is no assumption either way, but BAC data will be considered in court with other evidence. The driver may be convicted of DWI if the manner in which he or she is operating the vehicle implies that the individual is impaired.
	0.10% or more*	This is evidence of being under the influence of alcohol. Based on the BAC, the individual is drunk and can be convicted without further evidence.

*In California, Maine, Oregon, Utah, and Vermont, a BAC level of 0.08 percent defines intoxication. Georgia sets the BAC level defining intoxication at 0.12 percent.

Under this law, the driver agrees to submit to a BAC test in exchange for the privilege of driving. Refusal to take the test could result in immediate and automatic suspension of the driver's license, even if the driver is not guilty of driving under the influence of alcohol or other drugs.

Some states have instituted new laws to help reduce the availability of alcohol to those under age 21 and to diminish the chances that any teen would drink and drive. Provisions of these laws include:

- Suspension of driver's licenses for alcohol-related offenses
- Stricter laws against the purchase or possession of alcohol by minors
- Tough laws against the sale of false IDs to teenagers or the use of such IDs by teens
- Stricter laws against providing alcohol to minors
- Special restrictions on driver's licenses for those under 18, such as driving only during daylight hours or within certain distances of the driver's home.

Surviving victims of drunk-driving crashes and families of those who did not survive are entitled by law to try to recover their losses and be **compensated** for their pain and suffering. To achieve this, the wronged party brings a civil suit, which is separate from the criminal charges lodged by the state. The injured person bringing the civil suit can ask for money, other compensation, or actions to help make up for the injuries and losses caused.

In Your Community

1. How does your court system handle drunk drivers? Does it handle adults differently from juveniles?
2. Does your state have the implied consent law? Do you think this commitment to submit to alcohol testing is a fair exchange for the privilege of driving?
3. Recall the story of Susan Herzog. Her family filed a civil suit against the driver of the other car, who had been found guilty of DWI. The Herzogs sued for $1.5 million but agreed to settle for a proposal that the guilty driver pay them $936, $1 per week for 18 years (the length of Susan's life). The amount was to be paid on Friday, the day Susan died. Do you think this was a good penalty? Why or why not? How do you think the driver feels about the penalty? What other kinds of settlements in a civil suit might discourage drunk driving?

Drinking and Driving Facts

Although standard tests are used to measure blood alcohol concentration level and determine a possible violation of traffic laws, each person reacts to alcohol differently. Reactions often depend on how recently the person has eaten and on his or her mood and weight.

Because of these variables, no one can predict a "safe" number of drinks. The thing to remember is that alcohol is a drug, specifically a depressant, and it is better not to use it at all. Even small amounts slow physical reactions and thought processes.

Aside from this, there are some facts that everyone should know about drinking:

- Drinking coffee, taking a cold shower, or exercising will not help a person sober up.
- Time is needed for the body to rid itself of alcohol. For someone weighing 150 pounds, it usually takes about two hours for the alcohol from a single drink (12 ounces of beer, 8 ounces of a wine cooler, 5 ounces of wine, a one-and-a-half-ounce shot of liquor or a mixed drink) to leave the body.
- The faster an individual drinks, the more intoxicated he or she gets.
- Adding more mixer to a mixed drink so it won't taste as strong does not lessen the amount of alcohol.
- A can of beer contains just as much alcohol as a glass of wine or a shot of liquor. Don't think you won't get drunk because you're "only drinking beer."
- Fortified wines have a very high alcohol content. Some of them have at least as much alcohol in a single 12-ounce bottle as five shots of liquor or five bottles of beer.
- Wine coolers are extremely potent. They can contain 1.5 times as much alcohol as one beer.
- People don't have to be falling-down drunk before they create hazards. You might feel capable of driving when actually your driving ability has been seriously impaired by alcohol.
- Don't kid yourself by thinking that you'll "sober up" as soon as you get behind the wheel. Only time will help you become sober.

How Does Drinking Alcohol Affect the Driver Physically?

Using good judgment while driving means having the ability to think clearly and make quick, rational decisions. When operating a motor vehicle, judgment is needed to estimate speed, time, and distance accurately. Alcohol and other drugs impair that judgment. People may feel fully capable of driving when in reality their abilities have been greatly reduced.

A skillful driver must have many assets: good judgment, emotional control, good eyesight, and coordination. Drinking alcohol reduces ability in all these areas.

Because people cannot be sure how any amount of alcohol will affect them, drivers should not consider BAC guidelines as indicating how much drinking they can "get away with." The following rule makes the most sense: Drivers should not drink.

Almost 90 percent of the information a person uses while driving is delivered to the brain from the eyes. Even at low levels of BAC, alcohol causes muscles in the eyes to relax, resulting in a picture that is out of focus. Alcohol also reduces "glare vision" (which helps a person see when there is a quick increase in the amount of light) and "glare recovery" (which readjusts one's vision after the sudden increase in light). These abilities are especially important to driving at night, when many alcohol-related crashes take place. Side vision and the ability to judge depth or distance are also impaired by alcohol.

Your Turn

1. If you drank three beers in three hours, would you drive? What if you drank five glasses of wine in two hours?
2. You've been waiting all week for tonight. One of the football players is having a party, and you and your friends are invited. Your parents are letting you use the car. The party is in full swing when you arrive: Music is playing, beer is flowing, and everyone is having a great time. Someone hands you a beer. When you say, "No, thanks; I'm driving," everyone laughs. "What a wimp," "It's only beer," "Come on, chicken," you hear. You know that if you have one beer, it'll be difficult to stop, but you don't want to look weak. What would you do?

Common Signs of Drunk Driving

There are common signs that someone is driving while intoxicated. Many of these signs can also suggest other forms of impairment, such as drugged driving.

These danger signals include:

- Inability to control speed: moving too fast, speeding up or slowing down abruptly, driving slowly in the left lane

- Difficulty in making turns: running over the curb, going into the wrong lane
- Inability to keep the vehicle in position: weaving, straddling lanes, driving over the center lines
- Disobeying traffic controls: going through a yellow or red light, stopping for a green light
- Making quick or jerky starts
- Irregular stopping: stopping too soon before or too far after a stop sign, running stop signs, stopping where there is no stop sign or signal
- Irregular signaling: giving no signal, giving the wrong signal
- Poor use of the vehicle's lights: not using lights, failing to dim lights when appropriate.

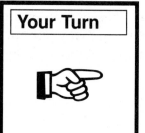

Your Turn

Read through the descriptions of the characters and the scenarios listed here. Then role-play the two scenarios and discuss the questions that follow.

Characters:

Vicki: You are a high school junior. Tonight you are going to a party on your first date with Mark, a senior. You have wanted to date Mark for a long time. You are worried about Mark meeting your parent. You know that your parent is very concerned about alcohol and other drugs at high school parties.

Mark: You are anxious to get to the party. You know that there will be alcohol available. You like to drink beer, but you know Vicki's parent will not let her go if there is any drinking.

Vicki's parent: You are worried about the teenage drinking and driving problem. You do not want Vicki to be put in any danger. You always meet and talk to the young men she goes out with before you let her go. You have never met Mark before.

Scenarios:

At Vicki's house: Vicki's parent and Mark are talking together for a few moments while Mark waits for Vicki to get ready. Vicki comes downstairs and says good night, and she and Mark leave for the party.

At the party: The party is out in the country, a long way from Vicki's house. Vicki is happy to be with Mark. The music is loud, and beer and wine coolers are available. Mark begins to drink. Vicki expresses concern but is told she's "too uptight."

The party continues and everyone begins to dance. Vicki drinks one wine cooler while Mark drinks beer after beer. The alcohol runs out and most of the guests decide to call it a night. Mark is obviously drunk, and Vicki is a little scared. Mark insists he can drive and gets into his car.

Role-play these situations: (1) the conversation between Mark and Vicki's parent while Mark waits for Vicki, and (2) the discussion that Mark and Vicki have about what is happening at the party and how they will get home.

Questions:

1. What questions might Vicki have asked Mark before their date?
2. What would you say to Vicki or Mark before they left if you were the parent?
3. Should parents refuse to let their teens go to parties where alcohol or other drugs might be present? Should parents expect teens to leave a party just because alcohol or other drugs are present?
4. How do you think Vicki and Mark dealt with her parent? Do you think they were honest about the situation? Why?
5. What could Vicki have done when confronted by Mark and others drinking at the party? What do you think she was concerned about?

Drunk drivers frequently are unable to keep their vehicles in position on the road. Weaving, straddling lanes, and driving over the center line are common signs of drunk driving.

6. What should Vicki have done about riding home with Mark? What choices did she have in this situation?

7. What if the party had been at Mark's house and his parents had left the house knowing that he and his friends would be drinking? Should Mark's parent be legally responsible for the drinking and any accidents the teens might have had on the way home?

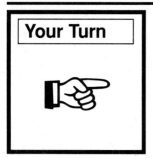

Your Turn

1. What would you do if you saw a car weaving down the road? Would it make a difference if you were driving a car or walking down the street? What would be your options? Would it make a difference if the driver were a friend?

2. Assume you are leaving a party and Lisa offers you a ride. As she begins to drive, you notice that she forgets to put on the lights and stops for a green light. What do you do?

3. You want to have a party. Your parents say no alcohol or other drugs will be allowed. Some of your friends say they don't think they'll come under these conditions. What will you do to make your party a success?

Community Responses

Groups have been organized all across the country to combat drunk driving and alcohol use by teens. One of the best-known groups is Mothers Against Drunk Driving (MADD), started by the mothers of children and teens killed in alcohol-related car crashes. The nearly three million women, men, and children who are members and supporters of MADD are involved in a number of educational and community awareness activities. In 1990, MADD had more than 400 chapters and around 30 community action teams throughout the United States. MADD chapters in many states were very active in the effort to get their legislatures to raise the drinking age to 21. This change in law, estimated by the National Highway Traffic Safety Administration to have saved 10,000 lives from 1982 to 1989, is a good example of what a community action program can accomplish.

Another group, with over 17,000 chapters in middle schools, high schools, and colleges, is called Students Against Driving Drunk (SADD). Besides encouraging young people to pursue a "no-use lifestyle," SADD encourages communication between parents and teens and promotes alcohol awareness programs in the community. The SADD "Contract for Life" between parents and teens reminds teens that their use of alcohol is against the law and spells out how teens who are endangered by drunk driving should call their parents for safe transportation home. Parents agree to provide such transportation and to postpone temporarily any questions or discussion. Parents also agree not to drive under the influence and to call home for transportation if necessary. Five million people have signed these contracts so far.

Young people who are members of MADD, SADD, or other anti-drunk-driving organizations have been involved in a number of community service projects. These projects help students meet peers who are interested in the same issues. Some of the school-based alcohol awareness activities that have proved successful include assemblies with expert speakers, poster or essay contests, and anti-drunk-driving floats for homecoming or other parades.

Chapters have also sponsored alcohol-free (sometimes called chemical-free) graduation, pizza, or dance parties, field trips, and other fun events. Fund-raising activities such as car washes, dance marathons, or the sale of shirts or stickers with the school logo have been used by many groups to support these events. Some groups also work with adult service organizations as volunteers for park cleanups, town fairs, dinners, fund-raisers, or other

Students Against Drunk Driving (SADD), which promotes community alcohol awareness programs, stresses communication between parents and teens.

activities. These are just some of the ways teen-led service organizations can make a difference in their communities.

**In Your
Community**

1. What is going on in your community and in your school to
   educate people about alcohol and drug-related injuries and
   deaths?
2. Are there active chapters of MADD, SADD, or other anti-
   drunk-driving groups in your community? How can students
   get involved?
3. What services are available in your community for teenagers
   with alcohol problems?
4. What would you like to do about the issue of drunk driving?

**Looking
Back**

You have been appointed to a special commission set up by your
school board to look at how to educate teens about drunk driving.
Although alcohol consumption under age 21 is illegal, teenage
drunk driving is still a big problem. You are considering two
approaches.

One approach aims to create pressure not to use alcohol, gives
teens facts about alcohol, and tries to build their self-esteem.
This approach encourages teens not to drink at all. Critics of this
approach say it is unrealistic, that some teens are still going to
drink, and that society must take this into account.

Another approach suggests that teens will decide for themselves
whether to drink or not based on the facts. This approach emphasizes
education concerning the requirements and penalties of the law,
the results of drunk driving, and how an accident or conviction
can hurt a teen's future. Critics of this approach feel that teens
must be given the clear message that drinking is illegal and will
not be tolerated.

Write a paragraph explaining the kind of approach you think
would be most effective and why.

11

Shoplifting

Words to Know

shoplifting
larceny
petit larceny
grand larceny
concealment
retailers
shrinkage
kleptomania

Objectives

As a result of this chapter you should be able to:

- Define shoplifting

- Identify common motives for shoplifting and the criminal consequences of this behavior

- Explain the impact of shoplifting on businesses, the general community, and teenagers

- Identify effective means of preventing shoplifting

What Is Shoplifting?

Shoplifting is a form of **larceny**, or theft. It is the crime of taking goods from a store without payment or the intent to pay. This crime is a problem for store owners because they lose money on each item that is not paid for by customers. Store owners make a living from the difference between the price they sell an item for and the price they paid to the company that made the item. The difference between these amounts, minus the owner's operating costs, is called profit.

Employee theft is a form of theft in which employees take things themselves, allow their friends to take things, do not charge for an item, charge a customer an improperly reduced price, or abuse an employee discount. Abusing an employee discount might involve using it to purchase merchandise for a friend.

Thefts valued at less than $100 are usually called **petit larceny**. This crime is considered a misdemeanor, sometimes carrying a

Shoplifting hurts retailers, who lose money on each item taken without payment.

fine and often a penalty of up to six months in jail. Thefts of a greater value are usually called **grand larceny**. Considered a felony, grand larceny often carries a fine and a penalty of up to five years in jail. Some states have a separately punishable crime called **concealment**, or attempted shoplifting.

Because shoplifting has so greatly hurt profits, many store owners now prosecute all shoplifters, even for first offenses.

What Is the Impact of Shoplifting on Businesses?

The 1989 *Uniform Crime Reports* (UCR) compiled by the Federal Bureau of Investigation (FBI) notes that about one out of every six larcenies reported to law enforcement in 1988 was shoplifting. The FBI also says that shoplifting increased by 35 percent between 1985 and 1989.

Reported incidents of shoplifting accounted for $3.6 billion in profit lost by retailers in 1988. **Retailers** are people or companies that sell goods to consumers for individual or household use. A 1989 Department of Justice study estimated that U.S. businesses of all types lose $40 billion each year due to employee theft.

The impact of shoplifting should be considered as part of the overall issue of **shrinkage**. This is the word businesses use to describe the percentage of profit that is lost to shoplifting, employee theft, and paperwork error. The amount lost to shrinkage is important to the consumer because the price that retailers charge for the goods in their stores is based on the expectation of a certain percentage of profit. If retailers lose too large a percentage of profit to shoplifting or employee theft, they are likely to have to raise prices in order to make up for that loss.

For instance, suppose the owner of a music store in your neighborhood bought 100 copies of a popular new cassette. The owner paid $500 ($5 apiece) for those cassettes and sells them for $750 ($7.50 each). Based on the definitions above, the owner expects

Figure 1–Average dollar amount shoplifted by type of store (per incident), 1991	

Department store	$ 165.00
Drugstore	$ 48.00
Mass/general merchandise store	$ 87.00
Specialty clothing store	$ 225.00
Supermarket	$ 107.00

Source: "An Ounce of Prevention," *Chain Store Age Executive*, January, 1991.

to make $250, less operating costs. If the owner loses 15 of those cassettes to shoplifters, $75 already paid out by the owner has been lost. These stolen cassettes represent $112.50 in income, or half the store owner's projected revenue. If more cassettes are taken, whether by shoplifters or employees, the owner might be forced to take action. Such action might include hiring a security guard, cutting back on the number of employees to reduce expenses, or raising prices.

Since business owners pay close attention to where their money is being made or lost, they are painfully aware of the costs of theft by customers and employees. According to the U.S. Chamber of Commerce, 30 percent of business failures in the United States are due to shoplifting.

Recent surveys of retailers indicate the following:

- One-half to three-quarters have problems with shoplifters.
- One-half to two-thirds pass all costs of shoplifting on to consumers.
- Two-thirds or more view teens as the most likely group to shoplift.

Your Turn

Consider the following situations and rate them from most serious to least serious. Then discuss your ranking with your classmates.

- A boy shoplifts candy and gum from a small store.
- A girl shoplifts expensive clothes from a department store.
- An older woman takes a bottle of perfume on impulse.
- A 12-year-old steals money from a parent to go to the movies.
- A 17-year-old boy who works at a fast-food restaurant gives his friends free hamburgers and french fries.
- A drug addict takes $50 from the cash register when the clerk is not looking.
- A sales clerk takes from her store a sweater that no one seems to want to buy.

1. What made you rank some of the situations as more serious than others?
2. If you saw any of these situations occurring, which ones, if any, would you report? To whom would you report?
3. Does peer pressure influence your responses? If so, why?
4. What is the impact of shoplifting on the shoplifter who is caught? On his or her family? On the community? On business? On law enforcement? On the criminal justice system?

Who Shoplifts?

According to Shoplifters Anonymous, most shoplifters are non-professionals who steal frequently from places where they regularly shop. In a 1984 survey conducted by a retail industry magazine, 9 percent of the shoppers surveyed admitted to shoplifting in the previous year.

A small number of people who steal many items frequently are responsible for a lot of the losses from shoplifting and employee theft. A 1990 retail industry survey revealed that shoplifters are caught 13 times as often as employees who steal. However, the dollar value of the items recovered from employee thefts is seven times greater than the value of items recovered from shoplifters.

There are five different types of shoplifters or employees who steal:

- Amateurs—people who steal on impulse or because they see an item they greatly desire. These people tend to believe that they will not be caught or sent to jail.
- Professionals—people who attempt to make their living by stealing from stores. They keep some of the goods and sell the rest.
- Drug addicts—people who steal to obtain the money they need to support their drug addiction. These people are committing a crime, but their main problem is drugs.
- Other desperate people—those who steal because they are in need of food or are otherwise economically or emotionally desperate. These people account for a very small portion of all shoplifting.
- **Kleptomaniacs**—a very small minority of shoplifters who have a mental disorder (kleptomania) that makes it extremely difficult for them to overcome their urge to steal.

Retail executives recently surveyed said they believe job stress, lack of adequate supervision or security measures, and job dissatisfaction are factors that contribute to employee theft.

Your Turn

The following are the five reasons most often given for shoplifting. Which do you think is given most frequently? Least frequently?

- Wanted "to get even" for high prices or other factors
- Did it "on a dare" from friends or acquaintances
- Did it "for a thrill" to see what would happen
- Did it on the spur of the moment just to get something
- Didn't have the money for what was wanted

1. First rank these reasons by yourself. Then get together in groups of three to four students and compare lists. Each small group should then come up with a list to share with the larger group.
2. Should society be interested in the reasons for shoplifting? Do any of these reasons justify shoplifting?
3. If you were a juvenile court judge, would knowing the reason someone shoplifted influence your decision regarding the case? If so, how? Should it influence your decision? Why or why not?

Costs of Shoplifting to the Community

Shoplifting is a crime with many costs. Some of the most significant costs to the community may include the following:

- The neighborhood store closes because the owner lost too much money to shoplifting.
- The store fires employees when it closes or lays them off because revenue is very low.
- The company that sells to the retailer loses either a customer if the store closes or a certain amount of business if the store reduces the number of items it sells.
- If the store closes, the truck driver who delivers the store's merchandise may lose a route or even his or her job.
- The neighborhood store's customers may have to travel farther to shop after the store closes.
- The remaining stores in the neighborhood may raise prices.

To curb shoplifting, retailers have taken security measures that add significantly to consumer costs. They have installed closed-circuit television cameras and other surveillance equipment, put electronic tags on items, hired guards and plainclothes security officers, established stricter refund policies, set up radio communication systems, and built in one-way glass panels that look like mirrors to monitor suspicious activity.

To cut down on employee theft, retailers and other business owners have taken such actions as setting clear policies regarding security and theft and providing more extensive employee training in security and waste prevention. In some cases, retail companies have begun to share profits with employees or to give them special bonuses for their help in reducing the amount of profit lost to shoplifting, paperwork error, and employee theft.

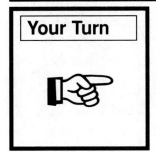

Your Turn

1. Assume you are the owner of a small grocery store in your city. Lately shoplifting has been increasing, and you are becoming concerned about losing your business. You believe that many teens who come in after school may be involved. List some of the costs involved in shoplifting.

   What actions could you take to protect your business from shoplifting? Are there any costs involved in these actions? How is shopping affected by the actions? What do these actions do to the store's atmosphere? What would the store's atmosphere be like if these measures weren't necessary?

2. Assume that you own a drugstore. The average value of items shoplifted from your drugstore is $48 per shoplifter (this is the national average for drugstores). If you have 10 shoplifters per day, how much money do you lose per day?

   To combat shoplifting, you hire a security guard at $80 per day. You want to adjust prices to cover the cost of shoplifting and the security guard. If you have 100 customers a day, each spending an average of $15, how much more will each customer have to pay?

How Does Shoplifting Affect Teens?

Teens, just like other consumers, are affected by the higher prices caused by shoplifters. Teens who work are also affected because the availability of jobs in stores is partly determined by the amount of money the owners can afford to set aside for employee salaries. If there are low revenues in the stores because of shoplifting, then there are likely to be fewer job opportunities for teens and others.

Teens who shoplift may also cause problems for their friends and classmates who want to shop or get jobs. Because some store owners see teens as people who are likely to steal, they may decide they do not want teen employees or shoppers in their stores.

The Price of Being Caught

Shoplifters face considerable risks. When salespeople or security officers catch shoplifters, they often call the police, who arrest the suspects and take them to the police station. Children and teenagers may be released to their parents' custody if it's their first offense. The case might be referred to juvenile court.

Everyone may find out about the arrest because police or court officers will often talk to the shoplifter's parents, neighbors, and school to make their report. If teens get caught shoplifting, their juvenile police records are supposed to be confidential and unavailable to future employers, but sometimes the information does get out.

Your Turn

A teenager is arrested for shoplifting at a department store. The teen's parents are called. They leave work and meet their child at the police station. All appear in juvenile court the next day. How will the teen feel? The parents? How will this incident affect the relationship between the teen and his or her family?

How Can Teens Stop Shoplifting?

Shoplifting can be reduced through community projects and education.

Teens and other members of the public must insist that shoplifting cease, must encourage honesty, must refuse to assist friends who try to shoplift, and must be willing to report any shoplifting they see.

Teens can be important partners in a coalition with retailers, shopping malls, chambers of commerce, civic clubs, community groups, law enforcement agencies, and the media to reduce this crime. As part of a team effort, you can:

- Organize school assemblies and classroom programs on the costs and consequences of shoplifting
- Put on skits, plays, and puppet shows that educate younger audiences about shoplifting
- Bring speakers to the school or operate a "teen speakers bureau" to address other teens, community meetings, civic clubs, and so forth
- Sponsor essay or poster contests
- Feature anti-shoplifting themes at school fairs or as part of special observances like Law Day
- Take field trips to businesses to learn what they must do to deal with shoplifting.

Your Turn

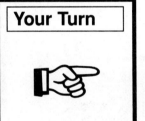

Assume you are the owner and operator of a clothing store. Most of your business is from customers in the local community. You have a shoplifting problem, and you know you may go out of business if your losses continue.

Penny and Geraldine are two local teenagers. They have just been caught in your store with goods you believe they tried to steal. You are sure that Penny is guilty of shoplifting because she had a $30 blouse with an electronic tag attached to it in her book bag. Geraldine had in her purse about $9 worth of unopened cosmetics that the store guard believes she took from a counter. But she says she bought these last weekend.

1. What are you going to do with Penny and Geraldine? Send them to the juvenile authorities? Return them to their parents? Give them a stern lecture?
2. Would you handle Penny's and Geraldine's cases in the same way? What would you do if Penny had been caught shoplifting in your store once before?
3. Would your experiences with Penny and Geraldine cause you to be concerned about having teenagers in your store?

Would you take action to prevent or discourage teens from entering your store?

4. What would you do if you were a customer in the store and saw Penny and Geraldine shoplifting? Would it make a difference if you knew them? Would your answer be different if they were good friends of yours?

In Your Community

1. Survey five or more students to get their opinions on shoplifting. Develop some questions to help you understand their opinions. What does your survey tell you about the causes of shoplifting and possible ways to prevent it?
2. What is the extent of the shoplifting problem in your community?
3. What is the estimated cost of shoplifting in your community?
4. What age group is most frequently charged with shoplifting in your community?
5. Are there any programs to curb shoplifting in your community?

Surveys can reveal what teens know about how and why shoplifting should be prevented.

| **Looking Back** | 1. Should teens who shoplift be treated differently than adults? What if a teen continues to shoplift? When, if ever, should a shoplifter be sent to prison or a juvenile institution?
2. Write a paragraph describing how you think the justice system should handle shoplifters. |

Appendix:
Designing a Project

Crime prevention projects can offer a community many opportunities for increased safety, service, and growth. Teens can organize, direct, and operate hundreds of activities aimed at other teens, younger people, particular apartment buildings, specific neighborhoods, or the community at large. Some of the many services teens can perform include educating the public about crime, starting neighborhood watches, conducting anti-vandalism campaigns, counseling other teens and younger children, and providing day care.

Crime prevention projects can be planned and carried out by classroom groups, school-based clubs, church youth groups, groups from community youth centers, and organized youth groups like Boy and Girl Scouts of the U.S.A. and Camp Fire Boys and Girls.

You might select a problem and an approach for solving it that are described in this book or that arise from classroom discussions of issues presented in "Your Turn" and "In Your Community" features. You might concentrate on a specific crime like vandalism or undertake a general awareness program.

How Do You Start?

Ask yourself these questions, and then ask them of a group of fellow teenagers:

- What problems do teenagers face in the community?
- What crime-related topics are of greatest interest and concern to teens?
- What community needs are going unmet?
- What organizations and institutions might be willing to join as partners in addressing these problems, topics, and needs?

● What resources might be needed to address the most urgent problems? Do we have those resources? If not, can we get them?

Your answers and those of your friends and classmates will go a long way toward helping you select the best problem(s) to target for action.

Planning

Once you've determined which problem(s) to address and your possible resources, you should undertake several key planning tasks:

Set Goals

Goals are the results you want from your program. They should be stated as positive aims for solving the problem.

Select Strategies

Strategies are the general approaches to be followed in order to meet your goals.

Specify Targets

Targets provide guidelines for your program's progress toward its goals.

Spell Out Tactics and Tasks

Tactics are the detailed steps by which strategies are implemented. They can include various activities, implementation methods, and refinements of strategies.

Tasks need to be assigned; assuming that "someone" will do a task practically guarantees that it won't get done. Also, people frequently accept assignments as a compliment to their ability, even though they might have been reluctant to volunteer their skills.

Plan Rewards, Feedback, and Evaluation

Rewards need to be direct and personal—not just community improvement, but recognition for participation and leadership. Rewards might include publicity, parties, ceremonies, plaques, or competitions.

Feedback is vital. Sometimes organizers forget that volunteers—teens as well as adults—have imagination, experience, and talent that could make the program more effective.

Evaluation involves determining whether you did what you planned, for whom you planned it, and the way you planned to. It is not an examination, but a learning device to help make future program changes.

Recruiting Resources

Once you've planned a project, you need human and material resources to carry it out. Much has been written about locating community resources for non-profit groups. Your local library probably has excellent references. But little has been said about recruiting teens to your program.

The most effective recruiting is based on the fact that people volunteer for programs that will help them meet their own needs and desires. Teen volunteers often cite these reasons for signing up for programs:

- To do something with friends
- To meet new friends
- To help victims of crime and others
- To learn new skills

- To explore careers
- To make school safer
- To help repay the school or the community for services they have provided
- To volunteer for the sake of volunteering
- To respond to a specific request for help from an individual or institution
- To list as an accomplishment on a college or job application
- To reduce crime against teens.

Use these reasons to help formulate effective appeals for volunteers.

Doing the Project

As you carry out your project, keep in mind these principles which can help ensure your program's success:

P Purposeful programs address real needs, are sufficiently structured, and are reasonably short-term.

A Agreed-upon ground rules should be determined for teens and adults.

R Roles that are diverse, as well as involvement at various levels, should be allowed.

T Tangible evidence of the program's serious intent should exist—a meeting room, a telephone number, a school credit.

I Instruction should be given to adults and teens in planning, organizing, speaking, and making decisions.

C Commitment by adults is important for meaningful youth participation.

I Involvement, rewards, and recognition—public and within the program.

P Pizza should be available periodically! Socializing and having fun can help the work go quickly.

A Adult leaders should keep their minds open to teens' ideas.

T Tangible evidence of the program's success should be made apparent—records of achievement, newspaper stories, testimonials.

E Energy and enthusiasm are prime ingredients for success!

Here are some types of projects you could undertake:

- Neighborhood watch—Residents keep an eye out for suspicious persons or activities, reporting them to law enforcement personnel.

- Operation Identification (Op ID)—In an effort to deter theft, people mark property with an identifying number and display a sticker warning that valuables are marked.
- Home security surveys—Students check areas in and around a house or apartment—doors, windows, locks, landscaping—to ensure that they are as safe and secure as possible.
- School crime watch/youth crime watch—Students report crime they observe in and around their school and promote school spirit and resistance to crime.
- Crime prevention clubs—Formed to help teens learn how to fight crime and protect themselves, clubs meet periodically to dispense information and to carry out specific crime prevention activities.
- Community cleanups—Citizens work together to clean up neglected and overgrown areas.
- Vandalism prevention—Young people use films, posters, and brochures to carry out a campaign that shows others the real costs of vandalism.
- Shoplifting prevention education—Students on their own or jointly with local businesses inform others of the costs and consequences of shoplifting.
- Student courts—Student judges, lawyers, jurors, bailiffs, and court clerks, under the guidance of local justice system experts, hear and try cases involving fellow students. Student courts are not mock courts—they hear real cases, make real judgments, and pass real sentences.
- Child protection education—Students present safety tips to elementary school children. Students can also teach drug and alcohol abuse prevention and vandalism prevention.
- Escort/check-in service for senior citizens—Members of youth groups accompany older citizens on errands. Students also make daily calls to senior citizens at pre-arranged times to make sure all is well.
- Youth forums and discussions—Forums, which help young people contemplate and contribute to the policies which affect their lives, can address security problems and take action to make schools and communities safer.
- Counseling (of peers and others)—Young people can help others through informal group sessions, scheduled appointments, or hot lines.
- Mediation—Teens can be trained as neutral third parties to resolve disputes peacefully among fellow students.

- Puppet shows and skits—Students can perform puppet shows for younger children and skits for peers dealing with issues from drug abuse prevention to latchkey children.
- Substance abuse counseling and prevention—Teens apply positive peer pressure on their friends by educating them about the prevention and reduction of substance abuse.
- Victim/witness assistance—Students can counsel teen victims, file compensation claims, accompany victims and witnesses to court, and inform victims and witnesses on how the court system works.
- Warm lines—Volunteers operate a telephone "warm line" during specified after-school hours to give children who are home alone safety tips, other advice, or just someone to talk to.
- Hot lines—Volunteers operate a telephone hot line, usually 24 hours a day, to assist people with immediate problems and crises.
- Fairs and displays—Young people can design creative educational displays for malls, schools, hospitals, businesses, and community centers, for the purposes of generating action for crime prevention and attracting new volunteers.

Your Turn

This exercise is designed to help you use the crime prevention information you've learned to practice developing a crime prevention program or project. It will provide good practice for planning your own project. Work in teams of three or four. Each team of should be assigned one of the three problems outlined by the Smallville Task Force at the end of the three fact situations listed. One team member should report each team's ideas to the entire group.

Each group should answer the following questions as part of its discussion:

1. Briefly define your audience. What message(s) do you want to send to that audience?
2. What resources—things and people—do you need? Brainstorm about where you might get some of these. Focus on two or three ideas.
3. What are the key responsibilities and how can they be divided up?
4. How will you know your program has worked?

You live in Smallville, a city of 45,000. The residents of Smallville acknowledge that some crime problems exist, but do not, in general, see their city as a hotbed of criminal activity. The Smallville Police Chief agrees that your city is fairly typical in its level of crime.

The city school system consists of two high schools, four junior high schools, and eight elementary schools. Your high school, Southside High, draws students from East and New Junior Highs, which draw students from Apple, Orange, Peach, and Banana Elementary Schools. There are about 1,500 students enrolled in grades nine through twelve at Southside High, which offers a variety of courses—college prep, business, and vocational.

The principal of Southside High is genuinely interested in young people and has, in the past, been open to innovations as long as they were well thought out and offered new ways to solve problems.

Schools in the Southside community have been hit by problems. Some amateur aerosol artists recently decorated the junior high school. On the same night, picnic tables and play equipment were damaged at Hillview Park.

It has been announced that two high school field trips, one for science students and the other for construction trade classes, are being cancelled because their funding had to be used to repair vandalism to area schools.

A Sidewinders' home basketball game against arch-rival Northwood had to be rescheduled as an away game because a person, or several persons, sawed through bleachers at the Southside gym.

A series of stories in the Smallville *Gazette* have reported the terror that Southside's Sidewinders strike in the hearts of many older people living near the school. One elderly widow, Mrs. Gresham, was quoted as saying, "I know not all the kids are bad, but it takes only one bad one to break my hip or ruin my roses or scare me out of my wits. I just don't leave the house when they're going to or coming from school." Many older people in the neighborhood have similar fears. The reporter pointed out that many of these people have little to live on, and therefore suffer badly when victimized by crime.

A recent meeting of the Chamber of Commerce made the local news when the chairman of the realtors' group warned that property values in the Southside neighborhoods are not rising to match those in other parts of town. In fact, according to him, Southside home values are actually falling. Why? Trash, graffiti, vandalized playgrounds at the parks and elementary schools play a large part. "Without good housing," Mr. Coldbanker warned, "Smallville cannot keep its industries and attract new ones, and all our property values will begin to suffer. Something must be done!"

1. The city needs some means of curbing vandalism to schools, elementary as well as junior and senior highs. This might include a "Watch" campaign (one way to teach young people about the costs of vandalism to them and to their parents), and/or cash incentives (a local businessman has made an offer) for preventing vandalism of school property.

2. Students don't like the idea that older people (in several cases their own grandparents) are terrified of them. They want to do something to make these older people less afraid—and to help them. Perhaps students can provide a service to help repair homes, an escort service to help with errands, or a call-up service to make sure those living alone are OK; or, seniors can volunteer in Southside's programs.

3. Several law enforcement, school, and community leaders feel that young people simply do not realize the seriousness of vandalism—he potential for injury, the economic costs, the costs in terms of broken equipment and lost opportunities like field trips. There must be some way to help all students learn about the costs of vandalism.

Glossary

Acquaintance rape the crime of forcing a person one knows to submit to sexual intercourse.

Active listening a communication skill that requires hearing and understanding a speaker, and then showing that you've heard and understood.

Addictive tending to cause habitual use or reliance.

Advocacy support for a cause.

Aggravating factor a circumstance that might raise the seriousness of an offense; the judge and jury might consider the existence of such a factor in deciding a case.

AIDS (Acquired Immune Deficiency Syndrome) the disease caused by the HIV virus that is transmitted from one person to another through sexual contact or the sharing of other bodily fluids, including blood.

Alcohol abuse the habitual misuse of alcohol (the most frequently abused substance).

Alcoholic a person who is addicted to alcohol; a sufferer from alcoholism.

Alcoholism the disease or condition of being addicted to the use of alcoholic beverages.

Amendment something that changes or modifies.

Apprehension the seizure or arrest of a person.

Arson the deliberate and malicious burning of property.

Assault an intentional physical attack; or, a threat of attack with the apparent ability to carry out that threat, so that the victim feels danger of physical attack or harm.

Bail money deposited with the court to have an arrested person released pending trial.

Blood alcohol concentration (BAC) the standard used to measure the amount of alcohol in a person's blood.

Booking the act of recording an arrest.

Burglary breaking into and entering a building with the intent to commit a felony.

Capital punishment the death penalty.

Child abuse the neglect or mistreatment of a child.

Coercion the act of forcing a person to do something against his or her will.

Compensation something, often money, given to make up for a loss.

Concealment the act of keeping someone or something from observation or discovery.

Conflict a hostile encounter between two or more people.

Conflict management a process used to resolve disagreements.

Confront to meet face to face.

Copyright violation the reproduction by any means (including photocopying) of substantial portions of the work of another person or group when that work is protected under copyright laws.

Crime a violation of a local, state, or federal law.

Crime prevention actions to reduce crime risks and build individual and community safety.

Criminal justice system the system that collectively ensures fair and regular procedures whenever criminal laws are violated.

Cross-examine to question a witness for the opposing side during a hearing or trial.

Damages the legal term for money paid to compensate for injury or loss.

Date rape the crime of forcing someone with whom one has a social engagement to submit to sexual intercourse.

Deceit misrepresentation, deception, trickery.

Defendant the person against whom a claim is made. In a civil suit, the defendant is the person being sued. In a criminal case, the defendant is the person charged with committing a crime.

Defraud to cheat someone out of property.

Disclosure the act of making something known, divulging something.

Discretion the exercise of judgment; caution about what one does or says.

Disputant one who is engaged in a dispute.

Drug abuse habitual misuse of a chemical substance.

Drug trafficking the sale of unlawful substances such as marijuana, cocaine, heroin, or other illegal drugs.

Drunk intoxicated, inebriated.

Embezzlement the taking of money or property by a person with whom it has been entrusted, like a bank teller or a company accountant.

Emotional abuse serious mistreatment of another person's feelings or emotional needs.

Environmental design measures that control access to, keep watch over, or manage a building with the purpose of reducing opportunity for personal or property crime.

Evidence information that tends to prove something.

Extortion blackmail; taking property by force or threat of harm.

Felony a crime punishable by a prison sentence of more than one year as well as by possible fines.

Forgery the making of a fake document or the altering of a real one with the intent to commit fraud.

Fraud any deception, lie, or dishonest statement made to cheat someone.

Gang a group, generally adolescents and young adults, involved in shared activities, many of which are violent or illegal.

Grand larceny (see *Larceny*)

Homicide the crime of killing a person; murder.

Impair to reduce in quality, to damage.

Implied consent law a driver agrees to submit to a blood alcohol concentration test in exchange for the privilege of driving. Refusal can result in immediate and automatic suspension of the driver's license, whether or not he or she is guilty of driving under the influence.

Incarcerate to confine, to imprison.

Incest intercourse between people who are close relatives.

Indeterminate sentencing a penalty in which a juvenile is released when found to be rehabilitated, rather than held for a specified time.

Indictment a grand jury's formal charge or accusation that a person has committed a criminal act.

Inhalants chemicals that produce vapors which are mind-altering when inhaled.

Intent the determination to do something using a particular method.

Interrogation questioning.

Intoxicate to make drunk.

Intravenous drugs chemicals that are injected into the bloodstream.

Kleptomania the persistent, neurotic impulse to steal, especially without economic motive, a rare psychiatric disorder.

Larceny the unlawful taking of another person's property with the intent to steal it. Grand larceny, a felony, is the theft of anything above a certain value (often $1,000). Petit larceny, a misdemeanor, is the theft of anything below a certain value (often $100).

Lobby to talk with or write to public officials (especially members of a law-making body) for the purpose of influencing legislation.

Mandatory sentencing a penalty in which the punishment is established by law with very little discretion left to the judge.

Mediation the act or process of a third party helping to reconcile a dispute between individuals or groups.

Mediator the neutral third person in a mediation.

Misdemeanor a criminal offense that is less serious than a felony and is punishable by a prison sentence of one year or less as well as by fines.

Neglect to fail to give care or proper attention to someone or something.

Options alternatives, choices.

Paranoia an irrational fear, suspicion, or distrust of others.

Peer pressure the influence that people of the same rank or age have on each other.

Perjury the act of testifying falsely under oath.

Perpetrator a person who does or performs some criminal act.

Petit larceny (See *Larceny*)

Physical abuse acts that cause physical harm or injury, particularly to a child.

Plea bargain to agree to plead guilty to a less serious charge in order to avoid being tried on a more serious charge.

Pornography writings and/or pictures intended to arouse sexual desire.

Probable cause the reasonable belief, known personally or through a reliable source, that a person has committed a crime.

Property crime the theft or destruction of something owned by someone.

Prosecutor the government's attorney in a criminal case.

Psychoactive mind- or behavior-altering.

Psychological dependency the condition in which a person feels that he or she needs drugs in order to cope with problems, function better in life, or feel different, whether there is a physical addiction or not.

Psychological intoxication a condition in which a person exhibits the emotional and behavioral characteristics of drunkenness without necessarily being drunk.

Rape the crime of forcing a person to submit to sexual intercourse.

Recognizance an accused person's promise that, without posting bail, he or she will appear at trial.

Rehabilitation an attempt to change or reform a convicted person so that he or she will not commit another criminal act.

Resolution the act of settling a problem or conflict.

Restitution a court order that requires a convicted person to repay the victim with money or other compensation.

Retailers people or companies that sell goods to consumers for individual or household use.

Revocation the act of cancelling something or taking permission away.

Robbery the unlawful taking of property from a person by force or by threat of force.

Search warrant an order issued by a judge giving the police power to enter a building in order to search for and seize items related to a crime.

Sexual abuse unlawful forced sexual contact and/or intercourse.

Shoplifting the stealing of articles from a retail business.

Shrinkage the percentage of profit lost to shoplifting, employee theft, and paperwork error.

Simple assault (See *Assault*)

Sober not drunk.

Software piracy the making of unauthorized copies of copyrighted software programs.

Substance abuse the misuse of chemicals that can alter the functioning of one's body and mind.

Triggers behaviors that cause anger in people.

Truancy the act of neglecting school, work, or duties.

Treatment the set manner of medical care for a person.

Vandalism the deliberate destruction or damaging of property.

Venereal disease an infection transmitted through sexual contact.

Venue the place where an alleged criminal activity took place.

Victim someone who is injured or killed or who suffers a loss as the result of action by another.

Victim impact statement information prepared for use in court that explains the effects of a crime on the victim.

Violent crime generally a murder, rape, robbery, or assault; a crime that involves threat or use of force.

Witness conference a meeting held to prepare a person to testify in court.

Index

Abuse
  alcohol, 132
  drug, 132
  substance, 132, 133-134
Acquaintance rape, 122-128
  effects of, on victims, 122-123
  prevention of, 126-127
Active listening, 99-100
Addiction, 132, 134-135, 139-140
Aggravated assault, 41, 49
Agreement, 94
AIDS, 133
Alcohol
  as cause of crime, 10
  effects of, on driving, 166-167
  and teens, 160-162
Alcohol abuse, 132
  effects of, 135-136
Alcohol-related offenses, 6
Amendment
  Eighth, 79
  Fifth, 77, 80, 82
  Fourth, 77
  Second, 57
  Sixth, 77, 81-82
Arguments, 92
Arson, 5, 62
Assault, 5, 40, 41, 49, 92
  aggravated, 41, 49
  conflicts as cause of, 50
  prevention of, 50
  protection from, 41-42
  sexual, 40
  simple, 41, 49
Auto theft, 5, 62

BAC (blood alcohol concentration), 161, 163-164, 167
BAC test, 165
Bail, 79
Blackmail, 62
Block watch, 19
Block watch, 66
Booking, of accused, 79
Brainstorming, 101
Burglary, 24, 61-62

Capital punishment, 89-90
  for juveniles, 90
Child abuse, 86, 108, 134
  causes of, 113
  characteristics of, 109
  disclosure of, 118
  emotional, 110
  incest as form of, 109
  neglect as form of, 110
  physical, 108
  prevention of, 115-117
  public opinion of, 111
  reports of, 111-112
  reporting, 117-118
  sexual, 108
  signs of, 114-115
  types of, 108-109
Child pornography, 108
Child protective service agencies, 112
Civil lawsuits, 74
Cocaine, 136
Community crime prevention, 11-12, 33
Community service, 19
Computers, and crime, 71-72

Concealment, 175

Confessions, 77

Conflict, 92

Conflict management, 50, 93-94

    personal, 93

    role of courts in, 95

    skills, 101

Conflict management process, 103-104

Conflict resolution, 94

Contraband, 77

Contract, 94

Copyright law, 71

Copyright violation, 62

Courts, *see also* Criminal justice system, 9

Crack, 136

Crime, 2

    causes of, 7-11

    and computers, 71-72

    costs of, 27-28

    definition, 4-5

    drug trafficking, 150-151

    effects of, on crime victims, 27-28, 30-32

    gang-related, 52-54

    handgun-related, 54-56

    holding offender accountable for, 19-20

    in the community, 13-14

    prevention of, 34

    property, 5, 27, 60, 61-62

    reduction of opportunities to commit, 19

    reporting of, 16-18

    types of, 5-6

    victimless, 67

    victims of, 2-4

    violent, 5, 27, 40-41, 54-56

    white-collar, 6

Crime prevention, 11

    community programs for, 11-12

    role of teenagers in, 13-16

Crime victims, 32

    advocacy groups for, 32-33

    assistance, 33-34

    compensation, 32

    elderly as, 24

    men as, 24

    organizations, 35

    rights, 32-33

    teenagers as, 24

    types of, 24-26

    women as, 24

Criminal justice, 74,

    costs of, 75

    process, 74

Criminal justice process, 75-76, 86-87

    bail and pretrial release, 79

    booking of accused, 79

    grand jury, 80

    juveniles in, 88

    looking for evidence, 77-78

    plea bargaining, 80-81

    preliminary hearing, 80

    pretrial motions, 80-81

    sentencing, 82

    trial, 81-82

Criminal law, 74

Crisis intervention services, 32

Cross-examination, 80

Damages, 74

Date rape, *see also* Acquaintance rape, 122

    causes of, 125-126

Death penalty, *see also* Capital punishment, 89

Defraud, 62

Delinquency, 86

Dependency, 134-135

    drug, 134

    psychological, 134-135

Disputants, 93-94

Dispute resolution, 93-94

Drinking age, legal, 162-163

Driving under the influence (DUI), 164

Driving while intoxicated (DWI), 164

Drug abuse, 132

    as cause of crime, 10-11

    as cause of violent crime, 51-52

Drug laws, 144-145

Drug trafficking, 148-156

    and other crime, 150-151

    consequences of, 151-153

    effects of, on the community, 154-155

    effects of, on teens, 148-149

    risks of, 149-150

Drugs, intravenous, 133

Drunk, 163

Drunk driving, 158

    and teens, 160-162

    community responses to, 170-172

    laws, 163-165

    signs of, 167, 169-170

Eighth Amendment, 79
Elderly, as crime victims, 24
Embezzlement, 62
Emotional abuse, 110
Environmental design, 68-69
Evidence, methods of looking for, 77-78
Extortion, 62

Family influence, as cause of crime, 9-10
Felony, 5
Fifth Amendment, 77, 80, 82
Forgery, 5, 62
Fourth Amendment, 77
Fraud, 6, 62

Gangs, 52-54
Graffiti, 52
Grand jury, 80
Grand larceny, 175

Handgun access, as cause of crime, 11
Handgun-related crime, 56-57
Handguns, 54
    restrictions on, 56-57
Home, protecting yourself in, 15-16
Homicide, 40
Hot pursuit, 77

Implied consent law, 164-165
Incarcerate, 19
Incest, 109
    characteristics of, 109
Indictment, 80
Inhalants, 136-137
Internal thefts, 24
Interrogations, 77
Intoxication, 158
    psychological, 161

Juvenile court, 86
Juvenile justice system, 74, 85-86

Kleptomaniacs, 177

Larceny, 5, 61, 174
    grand, 175
    petit, 174-175
Laws
    drug, 144-145
    status, 86

MADD (Mothers Against Drunk Driving;), 28, 30,
    170-171
Malicious mischief, 62
Mandatory sentencing, 82
Marijuana, 136
Mediation, 93-94, 103-104
    steps, 104
Mediator, 93-94
Men, as crime victims, 24
Miranda Warning, 77-78
Misdemeanor, 5
Moral values, 11

Neglect, 110
Negotiation, 93
Neighborhood Watch, 19, 70
    groups, 66-67
NOVA (National Organization for Victim
    Assistance), 32-33

Options, 101

Paranoia, 133
Parents of Murdered Children, 28
Patents, 71
Peer influence, as cause of crime, 9-10
Peer pressure, 139-140
Personal conflict management, 93
    skills, 96-97
    steps, 102-103
Petit larceny, 174-175
Physical abuse, 108
Plea bargaining, 80-81
Police protection, 9

Pornography
    as cause of crime, 11
    child, 108
Poverty, as cause of crime, 7
Preliminary hearing, 80
Pretrial motions, 80-81
Probable cause, 76
Property, 60
Property crime, 5, 60
    frequency of, 60-61
    invisible, 71
    prevention of, 66-67
    types of, 61-62
Prosecutor, 75
Public transportation, 44-45

Rape, 5, 40
    acquaintance, 122-128
    as victim of, 47-48
    date, 122
    myths and facts about, 124-125
    prevention of, 47-48
Reasonable doubt, 82
Receiving stolen property, 62
Recognizance, 79
Rehabilitation, 82
Resolution, 93-94
Restitution, 19-20, 82
Retailers, 175
Retribution, 82
Revocation, of license, 164
Robbery, 5, 24, 40, 60
    prevention of, 44-46
    protecting yourself from, 43-46

Search warrant, 77
Second Amendment, 57
Sentencing, 19, 82
    for juveniles, 88
    mandatory, 82
Sex offenses, 6
Sexual abuse, 108
Sexual assault, 40
    characteristics, 109
Shoplifters, 177
Shoplifting, 24, 174
    costs to the community, 178

effects of, on teens, 179
impact on business, 175-176
prevention of, 180-181
risks, 179-180
Shrinkage, 175
Simple assault, 41, 49
Sixth Amendment, 77, 81-82
Social problems, 20
Software piracy, 71-72
Status laws, 86
Street crime, 41-42
Students Against Driving Drunk (SADD), 170-171
Substance abuse, 132
    cost of, 138-139
    effects of, 133-134, 135-137
    prevention, 143-144
    signs of, 141-142
    trends among teens, 137-138

Teenagers
    as crime victims, 2-4, 24, 63-64
    role of, in crime prevention, 13-16
Television influence, as cause of crime, 11
Theft
    employee, 174
    prevention, 65-66
    shoplifting, 174
    victims, 63-64
Trial, 81-82
Triggers, 97-98

Unemployment, as cause of crime, 7

Vandalism, 5, 62, 67
    costs of, 67-69
    prevention of, 68-70
    victims of, 67-69
Venue, change of, 81
Victim, *see also* Crime victim, 24
    rights, 32-33
Victim advocacy groups, 32-33
Victim compensation, 32, 165
Victim impact statements, 82
Victims for Victims, 28
Victims of crime, rights, 75
Victims of theft, teenagers as, 63-64

Victim/witness agencies, 79
Victim/witness assistance, 33-34
Victim/witness intimidation, 79
Violent crime, 5, 40-41
   and drug abuse, 51-52
   frequency of, 60-61
   gangs as cause of, 52-54
   and handguns, 54-57
   linked with drug abuse, 51-52

White-collar crime, 6
Women, as crime victims, 24